Sneaking
Out

◆

SOUTHWESTERN WRITERS COLLECTION SERIES
Connie Todd, Editor

The Southwestern Writers Collection Series originates
from the Southwestern Writers Collection, an archive and
literary center established at Southwest Texas State University
to celebrate the region's writers and literary heritage.

Sneaking Out

◆

Prudence Mackintosh

UNIVERSITY OF TEXAS PRESS, AUSTIN

Requests for permission to reproduce material from this work should be sent to
Permissions, University of Texas Press, P.O. Box 7819, Austin, TX 78713-7819.

∞ The paper used in this book meets the minimum requirements of
ANSI/NISO Z39.48-1992 (R1997) (Permanence of Paper).

Library of Congress Cataloging-in-Publication Data

Mackintosh, Prudence.
Sneaking out / Prudence Mackintosh.— 1st ed.
p.   cm. — (Southwestern Writers Collection series)
"Some of these chapters have appeared, in slightly different form, in *Texas
Monthly*"—Verso t.p.
ISBN 0-292-75234-2 (cloth : alk. paper)
1. Parent and teenager—Anecdotes.   2. Teenage boys—Anecdotes.
3. Parenting—Anecdotes.   4. Family—Anecdotes.   I. Title.   II. Series.
HQ799.15 .M29 2002
649 '.125—dc21   2002004778

For

Sue Varner

Mary Kay Storey

Patty Herd

Becky Crouch Barrales

Nancye Hudgins Briggs

Charlene Kline Marsh

Judy Duke

and all the other brave mothers
whose sons' early leaving
made me hug my own so close.

Contents

◆

Preface

◆

In my late twenties and through the decade of my thirties, I wrote with some frequency and urgency about my experiences with family life. The writing was "urgent" because I had so few hours to do it. Some of it was scribbled standing up in the kitchen. The first book, *Thundering Sneakers,* chronicled my life with growing toddlers, revealing my great expectations and, frequently, grave misgivings. The second book, *Retreads,* carried the family of five (in which I am the only female) rather quickly through the years leading to adolescence.

This third volume on the domestic scene has been long in the making, though not for lack of material. Life with teenagers and young adults is far richer than life with inarticulate, lisping toddlers. The letting go and their breaking away is only part of the story. These are also the years of being stretched thin between two generations. I had to remember to pick up my own prescriptions before driving three hours to my hometown to pick up my parents' prescriptions, and often stopped halfway (Sulphur Springs) to call the reluctant scholar in Austin to remind him that Thursday was the last day for crucial "drops" and "adds." These years kept me scribbling as furiously as the seemingly endless housebound days of toddlerhood once did.

Time with children speeds up mightily about age twelve, however. They seem to go from twelve to twenty-one in half the time it took them reach six. Trying to capture these fleeting adolescent moments on paper presented several problems. Who needs a mother publishing color commentary on his teenage years? I declined a book contract in 1985 when my favorite characters turned fifteen, thirteen, and nine, respectively. If I'd had daughters, I probably would have had to close up shop much earlier. My boys never protested what I wrote about them; they never read it. They did inquire, from time to time, if I was making enough money with my typing to buy them a motorcycle. They are now grown men living elsewhere who write well enough to pen a Mommie Dearest on me if I fail to respect their privacy. I could probably still buy them off with a motorcycle, though.

Why write this book at all? I have little advice to offer beleaguered parents except, once again, the solace of shared experience. My children sometimes behaved preposterously. So did I. I continue to believe, however, that life is richer and perhaps more understandable if I can wrestle it to the page. These are the years when as a parent, one moves from nurture to nature, finding great comfort in theories of unalterable, genetic disposition. How I loathed as a young mother hearing that a dour Scottish strain ran in my husband's family that I would be powerless to change. How accepting I am of that idea now.

What I know and write about my children during these

years is, of course, suspect. Every parent of teenagers knows how the fun-house mirror can suddenly tilt with a phone call from school, a message left on an answering machine, or a policeman's knock at the door. Suddenly, all that you had perceived about your healthy, well-adjusted, law-abiding child is called into question. I sometimes think that this is the first generation that has sheltered their parents—or needed to.

My sons have been remarkably forthright with me, asking my advice on subjects that I could never have broached with my own parents. And yet there is much that I do not know about them. (Probably much that I do not want to know or certainly should not know about them.) Nevertheless, boys are careless. They leave things in their pockets. Stuff tumbles out of their backpacks and rolls under the bed. They write letters full of what one hopes is teenage braggadocio to their friends and save them under irresistible titles in my computer. Their English teachers often required them to write personal journals at school, and I found those disturbing revelations (or was it fiction, designed to "smoke" the snoopy English teacher?) tossed in the trash basket at the end of the term. If they had been more diligent about taking out the trash, I would have known less. I never steamed open their mail. College acceptance and rejection letters can be read through the envelope if held up to a sunny window.

On the other hand, I have always felt that notes, letters, receipts, and other items left fully exposed on the floor next to smelly socks or in jeans pockets that I had to empty for laundering were fair game as long as I kept the non-life-threatening information to myself. It wasn't always easy to pretend to be clueless.

Many times, however, we were clueless. Recently, over dinner one evening, my husband and I declared that the statute of limitations had run on things that happened in high school. This announcement elicited the *real* story of the dent in the side of the car circa 1985. How had I kept a straight face when the three of them explained that year that they had just been taking turns tossing the garden hoe like a javelin trying to dislodge two basketballs caught in the goal net when the hoe escaped someone's grasp and slammed into the side of the car? It seemed plausible to me, since none of the three had a driver's license in '85. "Duh, Mom . . ."

These were the years when the brothers began to speak in apparent non sequitur code. If I hadn't seen the movies *Spinal Tap* and *Raising Arizona,* I would have thought they'd all had strokes. After a decade of trying to rip each other's ears off, they declared a physical truce (never a verbal one) and closed ranks on their dad and me. It enabled the youngest to say tantalizingly when the two older ones were in high school, "You think you know about my brothers. You think we're all nice boys. You know NOTHING."

I never said they were nice boys. That was their Grandmother Jane.

Prudence Mackintosh
DECEMBER 2001

Sneaking Out

Out

◆

Homework

◆

"We never expected you to set the world on fire academically," my own mother said when I called in 1963 to tell her that I had just received a midterm failing notice in a math course at the University of Texas. Her refusal to be outraged so infuriated me that I located a tutor and by the end of the term earned a B in the course.

I've never asked her if her response was calculated. I doubt it. My parents and their contemporaries were the last of the real grown-ups. Having lived through the Depression and World War II, they were not inclined to lose sleep over my brother's or my unfinished algebra homework, assist with science projects, or consider our school lives, beyond deportment, to be any reflection on themselves. School was our business. And we muddled through, assuming full credit for whatever successes we achieved—or at least not blaming our parents for our failures. We were the products of what I affectionately call "benign neglect," a parenting mode now decidedly out of fashion.

In our attempt to be good parents, my generation has assumed, with ample encouragement, that what our children need most is us at their sides engineering and applauding their successes. It's a peculiar stance for parents who recall their own early independence with some pride. "We had private lives even in elementary school because our parents didn't transport us everywhere we went," one friend recalls. "I walked or rode my bike or took the city bus to places she never knew about." Another friend remembers that her mother bought only one box of her Girl Scout cookies. "I spent half a day on the telephone selling my own daughter's cookies and then bought the carton that I couldn't sell. Why am I doing this?"

I swore off doing the kids' homework the night we all stayed up until 2 A.M. cutting up *National Geographics*, weekly newsmagazines, and probably the encyclopedia to complete a sixth-grade notebook entitled "Australia A to Z," which contained an illustrated "Down Under" fact for each letter of the alphabet. I confess that I had previously researched, coauthored, and illustrated a seventh-grade effort on Australia's Great Barrier Reef. With such expertise, I moved our midnight project from "aborigine" to "nudibranch" with some alacrity. At "P is for pygmy python starfish" I got a little surly, and by the time we reached "W is for wallaby" I quit and started recalling the lack of gratitude for my assistance in compiling a sixth-grade FBI dossier on Ulysses S. Grant. (This project included my handcrafted replica of Grant's movable false teeth and eyeglasses.) Had no one even saved my fourth-grade poem on Columbus in perfect tetrameter written at the breakfast table just moments before the tardy bell?

Like many parents in my neighborhood, I have been through what we once called junior high four times, once for myself and again for each of my sons. I have no advanced degrees for these extra years of classwork, but I do have a measure of expertise in Maya civilization, the Ku Klux Klan, and algebraic trains that pass in the night while traveling in opposite directions at varying speeds. My magnum opus, however, is a seventh-grade Alamo diary containing paper that I soaked in tea and coffee grounds, dried in the oven, burned around the edges, and finally stained with blood from my own finger.

I know that I am not alone in these dubious achievements. One has only to browse the beribboned projects at the school science fair to grasp the commitment some parents have made. "Gone back to graduate school?" I jest upon seeing a mother combing the children's encyclopedia at the neighborhood library in the middle of the day. This phenomenon is not limited to my neighborhood. Any enclave of high-achieving parents is susceptible. A Houston friend tells me that she once calligraphied a five-generation family tree for her son in one night. "Since he gave me no advance warning, I had to borrow a family from an elderly neighbor down the street who is into genealogy," she confided. In still another neighborhood, a mother admits to spending an entire weekend trapping insects for her son's bug project. "Well, what else could I do? He just schlepped around with a mayonnaise jar for an hour and came up with two cockroaches and some fleas off the dog. I've seen the bug displays at the school before. This is the big leagues. Some parents will have ordered exotic South American butterflies and they'll have them displayed on imported vegetation."

She's right about the South American butterflies. This competitiveness among parents knows no bounds. When Jack was six years old, his crudely painted homemade racer careened off the track at Indian Guide Derby Day, while other slick, streamlined, professionally weighted models sped straight for the finish line. We knew then that a kid's solo effort wasn't going to win any ribbons in this environment.

Kids don't solo very often around here. Parents transport them amazingly short distances. "I drive her to high school on humid days," admits one mother. "Her hair falls if she has to walk from the student parking area, so I drop her off at the door." Parents in our neighborhood serve the food in the school lunchrooms not only in elementary school but right on through high school. We line the sides of the soccer fields and basketball courts after school, and sometimes cause the children's games to be forfeited because of our overzealous involvement. Attendance at Friday night high school football games is a Texas tradition, but parents in my neighborhood pack the daytime pep rallies as well. The children perform their trial-and-error rituals of growing up in the presence of a very supportive but also inescapable audience.

In the realm of schoolwork, parental involvement is so prevalent and so taken for granted that I sometimes wonder if teachers can assess the naked capabilities of their students. Accordingly, assignments seem to have escalated in complexity, as if the instructor presumes a backup staff of researchers, graphic artists, writing coaches, and word processors. The McKenzie family will never forget their son's ninth-grade science project, which involved his electrically shocking herds of roaches through a maze. "I think he ground up the 'smart' roaches and fed them to a new control group of roaches to see if the learned behavior could be transmitted through cannibalism," the mother recalls. "The paper that accompanied it required much poring over the works of B. F. Skinner and several trips to the medical school library. We were so let down when he received a B. The teacher said his charts and graphs weren't good enough." I think I would have demanded a Nobel committee review.

Similarly, mothers of sixteen-year-olds discuss the use of leitmotiv in Mark Twain's *A Connecticut Yankee in King Arthur's*

Court. "There must be more parents with advanced degrees in literature in this neighborhood than I thought," my friend Anne told me. "I have my master's, and I only made a C."

Things weren't always this way. The only parental help I can remember getting on a paper in high school was my mother's driving me from my hometown, Texarkana, to the Shreveport Public Library so that I could do research on early American abolitionists and suffragettes. Why we thought a Louisiana library would enlighten me on either topic is, in retrospect, puzzling, but I do remember thinking it was a remarkable gesture on my mother's part. Now I hear tales of a father who has a modem hookup to his son's personal computer at college so that he can assist the boy for four more years.

Parents get hooked into these performances in a number of ways. The schools consciously or unconsciously encourage it. The recent clamor for more homework as a part of school reform casts parents in the role of study hall supervisors. If the homework is anything more than rote drill or busywork, it may unfairly extend the parent's role to teacher. When our teaching skills are inadequate, we either become generous collaborators or feel guilty when our children do poorly. Parents begin to feel that they are being graded instead of their children.

A woman with a son in private school laments, "My son recopied his report on ancient Egypt four or five times because the teacher stressed that it had to be 'perfect.' When he received a D because it had three misspelled words and a punctuation error, I headed for the principal. 'This can't be a D paper,' I said. 'He did his research thoroughly, organized it all by himself, and it seems well written for a sixth grader.'

"'You should have proofread it,' the principal said.

"'I did proofread it. Does my child get a D because I can't spell "pharaoh"?'"

Of course parents are reacting to their own peer pressure. One parent's typing his sixth grader's report can send a whole neighborhood of parents to their computers. At the middle school's open house, an eager mother asks, "Would it help if I laminated some flash cards and drilled him for his vocabulary test each week?" The next day there's a run on index cards at the office supply store. A professional decorator adds a few touches to the pumpkin art contest. An engineer consults on and finally designs a simple pulley device for a third-grade science lesson. A professional writer edits a college admissions essay. Once the ante is upped, independent student effort looks shabby by comparison. One must admire the wit and courage of the child who, when asked to make a soil table for his geology unit in science class, assessed the projects prepared by parents of his classmates and then unveiled his own four-legged mud-pie table.

In addition to the parental peer pressure, I think the inflation of expectation from society also pulls parents into schoolwork. Private schools brag to their alumni that the alumni could no longer meet the current entrance standards. The much-quoted statistic that 96 percent of our local school system's students go to college is both heartening and intimidating. "What if my child is in the other four percent" is not the only fear; among competitive parents who set unreasonable goals for themselves (exercise classes at 5 A.M., indeed), the question may be, "What if my kid is not in the top ten?" In many households, "no pass, no play" is translated to "no A, no play." One parent confides, "More tutors are working with Ivy League–bound honor students in this neighborhood than with the kids who really need help." In an insecure parent's quest to measure "How'm I doin'?" on the fast track, the kid's class rankings and ultimately his college acceptances are important mileposts.

It's not always their own ego involvement that drives parents to get tangled up in schoolwork. Some admit that their children are so overscheduled after school with drill teams, athletics, ballet, church activities, music lessons, and Scholastic Aptitude Test prep courses that they honestly don't have enough hours in the day to do it all alone. "I sort through her assignments every day and tackle what I consider the busywork myself—the map coloring, the poster lettering, and the magazine cutting," one weary mother told me. "The substantive work is up to her."

Then again, some of us are just former schoolteachers who recognize the limitations of a teacher with thirty students. We see holes in our children's education. We teach our own children to diagram sentences so they'll know when their infinitives are split. We nail maps on the breakfast room wall when geography gets lost in social studies. We are frustrated when our children make pedestrian trudges through poems, novels, and plays that we believe have soul-searing power. "I want him to know that there is more to history than dry facts and multiple-choice exams," says one mother. I see her at the local library with biographies of Thomas Aquinas and Martin Luther. She checks out videos of *The Lion in Winter* and *A Man for All Seasons* in hopes that she can make it all come alive for her kids.

Particularly vulnerable are single parents, although many tell me that they're just too exhausted to take on their children's homework burdens. "If my kid fails, people will say it's because we messed him up emotionally," a recently divorced mother said. Extra guilt and an emotional need to be needed ensnare the single parent as well.

One doesn't have to be divorced, however, to want to extend the nurturing role well into high school. The old intimacy between mother and son that threatens to disappear completely in the teenage years is sometimes briefly rekindled while burning the midnight oil together and scrambling to get a paper finished. "He seldom thinks I have the answers to anything anymore," another mother confided, "but when it comes to sonnet form, an explication of an Emily Dickinson poem, or a Latin translation at midnight, he has nowhere else to turn."

Some of my contemporaries insist that their involvement with their children's schoolwork is a rebellion against the benign neglect of the fifties and early sixties that I now look on with some affection. "My parents never took me to see any colleges or encouraged me to look at the catalogs," one woman says. "I accepted going to the state university as if there were no alternatives. If someone had just held out a dream for me— showed me that my scholastic ability had some door-opening power beyond the National Honor Society, I might have. . . . Well, I'm devouring my sons' college catalogs as if they were best-sellers and fantasizing about the kind of life that might spring from four years in Massachusetts, Virginia, or even California. I don't want my children ever to say, 'Why didn't you make me . . . take me to see . . . tell me about . . . ?'"

The bottom line in success-oriented neighborhoods like mine is that failure isn't permitted. And failure is narrowly defined as anything short of perfection. Although my own parents seemed inclined to regret but accept any shortcomings in their offspring—stupidity, lack of gumption, or laziness—the more affluent parents of my generation seem bent on remedying or removing every possible imperfection. We are afflicted with a sort of cosmic hubris brought on by a host of experts who assure us that if we buy enough books or attend enough seminars we can raise a brighter child, develop a positive attitude, create a lifelong reader, keep our children drug free, get them into the right college, and guarantee them a painless, successful life.

We are cautioned to retain our sons who have summer birth-days an extra year in kindergarten to give them a running start in academics and perhaps an advantage on the athletic field. We straighten their teeth, pin back their protruding ears, and erase their acne. Perfecting their academic performance is more of a challenge. We employ child psychologists when they mys-teriously lack motivation. One mother admitted to me that the only result of her motivational efforts was the refining of her own ability to make charts on her children's behavior. We also subject our kids to expensive diagnostic tests to discern aptitudes or to give failure a more acceptable name. I can't imagine my own mother keeping a straight face on being pre-sented with a diagnosis of ADD (Attention Deficit Disorder). But then, she wouldn't be tempted to purchase a book titled *The One-Minute Mother* to remedy it, either.

My oldest son, Jack, always our noble experiment, once endured a battery of tests, which he now refers to as that "retard weakness show up test." "Thanks to that test, Mom," he says, "I always remember when I sit down to study for a history exam that I have difficulty memorizing unrelated facts." (Who doesn't?) From this unfortunate experience, I conclude that it's impossible to subject a child to any kind of tests without implying that something is wrong with him. William, the youngest, clung to the notion for years that he was a little deaf just because I had his ears tested at the Callier Speech and Hearing Clinic after a winter of ear infections.

Even when real failure, not just imperfection, is an unavoid-able fact, we scurry to soften the blow. One culpable parent confessed to me, "When Alex flunked Spanish at our public high school, the prospect of summer school looked so bleak that we decided to send him to Phillips Academy (Andover) summer school to make it up. After a week of orientation in Massachusetts, the actual school was held in Cuernavaca,

Mexico. To top it off, we had hosted a Spanish exchange student in our home that year, and his family insisted that we allow Alex to spend the month of August with Roberto in Spain. My husband called from the office one afternoon and said, "I'm about to write a check for four thousand dollars to pay for Alex's summer. I just wanted to be sure that this is the way we intended to punish him for failing Spanish."

We are more fearful of failure in our children's lives than previous generations were. We have been cautioned since our children were born that we must bolster their self-esteem with lots of positive strokes. Psychologists tell us to correct the behavior, not the child, and to relieve their stress and anxiety by listening to them nonjudgmentally. As a result, we have come to view our children as incredibly fragile creatures. When the doors to their rooms slam in anger or frustration over schoolwork, we are the first generation of parents to lie awake wondering if they will take drugs or commit suicide. Letting them sink or swim was easier when the consequences of sinking were not so dire.

As parents, however, we can assume total responsibility for their emotional health only at the expense of our own. Kids are notoriously fickle worriers. They casually drop anxiety bombs like "I'm failing math" on us. We spend most of the night studying quadratic equations and the next afternoon locating a tutor, only to have the child respond blankly a day later, "Tutor? Oh, I don't need one. She curved the test."

Common sense suggests to me that our children are better served in their progress toward maturity by seeing real adults leading reasonably adult lives. Adults do not have lengthy conversations in the evening about associative and distributive math properties. They learned the location of the Cape of Good Hope years ago and perhaps can get on with adult thoughts about the plight of South Africa and the novels of Nadine

Gordimer. They read their home readers in 1952 and now can indulge themselves in the Sunday *New York Times* on a winter's evening. They wrote their own papers in 1963 and now earn money, not grades, with the skills they acquired. They met each other in college, and while the kids are busy with their homework, these adults would like to get reacquainted.

If we are always supplying our children with creative ideas, instant answers, library books, and an overlay of presumably superior adult effort, we are denying them the pleasure of discovery and serendipitous sidetracks so essential to intellectual development. We are also shielding them from honest assessments of their own work at a time in their lives when learning from mistakes could be the beginning of wisdom.

But common sense in child rearing is as uncommon as consistency. I remember lying awake worrying more about the concluding sentence for William's third-grade paragraph on snakes than I worried about the lead for my own article. Jack lightened my load by going to boarding school when he was fifteen. Drew relieved me of his homework duties shortly after the Australia episode when I became maniacally obsessed with getting him organized. "When your mother buys a three-hole puncher, you're in trouble," he groaned.

During a recent exhibition of kites at our local art museum, the kitemaker was asked by an adult in the audience, "But how do you *make* a kite fly?"

"You can't," said the kitemaker with a mischievous grin, knowing that her audience is accustomed to control.

Nor can we make our children fly, even with nagging, prodding, and a dozen fix-it clinics for study skills and time management. We can adjust the harnessing and add longer tails, but if they fly at all, they will be borne aloft on mysterious winds that we can neither control nor predict.

Canterbury Tails

◆

In the summer of 1985, my best friend, Elizabeth, and I, with some help from our husbands, prodded an enormous, unwieldy, many-legged beast through London and the English countryside. On a given morning the beast's front paws (William, eight years old) were already at the Bond Street Station eagerly awaiting a train to the Changing of the Guard at Buckingham Palace. The belly of the monster (Drew, twelve years old) lollygagged in the hotel dining room, oblivious to the cost of hot chocolate refills. The lethargic reptilian hindquarters (Jack, my fifteen-year-old and Elizabeth's sons, Patrick and Charlie, fifteen and sixteen) lounged in bed alternately playing poker and watching endless cricket matches on the abysmal flickering black-and-white telly. For two weeks, four parents ran the length of the beast, restraining the eager front paws, coaxing the belly away from the table, and viciously forking the hindquarters out of bed. Where was Saint George when I needed him?

The small hotel met our travel brochure expectations downstairs—charming dining room and numerous antiques-filled sitting rooms for tea or cocktails in the afternoon. Upstairs, however, our tiny rooms' single windows opened onto an airless shaft in the dark middle of the hotel. London was experiencing a heat wave, and of course the hotel was unair-conditioned. Through the open window, which gave little relief from the heat, we heard every intimate utterance, every toilet flush. The boys' rooms seemed nicer, but they confided days later that one of their toilets never flushed.

After a brief walk around the city, Jack announced, "There is nothing here that I couldn't see in the U.S., except the British part of the Live-Aid concert, which I'm going back to the hotel now to watch." None of the children accompanied us that evening to the Hyde Park Serpentine to celebrate Handel's 300th birthday outdoors with the London Philharmonic. Spectacular orange comets ascended with the rising trumpet melody of the composer's Water Music and exploded in baroque splendor over the water with uncanny synchronicity. It was one of the great moments of my life, a performance fit for a king— but not, perhaps, for a fifteen-year-old.

We had anticipated that traveling with five boys might mean more burgers at Wimpy's than we wanted. Despite my sermons on travel and the opportunity to feast on the astonishing oddness of the world, the hindquarters and the belly located a Pizza Hut run by an Indian family in the heart of the city and never dined with us again. The youngest accompanied us to dinner each evening, but exhausted from the lengthy walking that all our outings entailed, he frequently passed out before the main course was served. I have vivid memories of his sleepy, heavy head falling forward into a bowl of minestrone in a posh Italian restaurant.

Even the days when we got the whole beast up and running toward the same destination were not what we'd envisioned. Shepherding five boys through the streets of London and the various tube stations left Elizabeth and me shell-shocked at the end of the day. The boys did not walk any-where. If they were behind us, they stepped on our heels. If in front of us, they raced too far ahead. Sometimes running backward, they dashed into the roadway, forgetting to look for traffic on the "wrong" side of the street. The youngest whined that he could walk no further, but then raced to catch up with the older boys, who now jumped on and off double-decker-bus platforms at busy intersections just for the hell of it. They dragged their hands along sooty buildings and wrought-iron railings and wiped them on my oatmeal-colored cardigan when they leaned on me to catch their breath in the train station. They tried to touch speeding trains as they passed and made karate moves on each other with their backs to the empty tracks. Once the rush-hour crowd pushed and shoved us, filling the train car so quickly that four of the boys were relegated to another car. We worried that we'd never see them again. Then we worried that we would.

They charged straight through the Tower of London in search of the crown jewels. No Beefeater guide for them. They missed the edifying tales of bastard pretenders beheaded by unskilled executioners. "Took 'im seven whacks to get the head off, it did." I was glad to be alone in the light and airy St. John's Chapel. What would the hindquarters care about such a perfect specimen of Norman architecture? When I caught up with them, they were speculating on how King Henry peed when he was all suited up in his armor.

They donned their Walkman headphones to drown out the spirited bus tour guide's spiel on Dickens's England.

I had a plan for slowing their pace through the British Museum. Bribery. I handed each boy a sort of scavenger hunt quiz and promised a one-pound coin for the correct answers:

1. Where did the Elgin marbles come from? When?

2. What's so hot about the Lindisfarne Gospels?

3. Find a cat with earrings.

4. Find a mask, shield, and helmet from a Saxon ship. Describe it.

5. Who is the better speller, Mary Queen of Scots or Elizabeth I? Give examples.

6. To what does Elizabeth I compare herself in a letter to her young stepbrother?

7. Draw your favorite mummy.

Elizabeth and I began our leisurely stroll through the museum, confident that we had them occupied for at least half a day. Wrong.

They returned in forty-five minutes with the quiz minimally but correctly filled in. A guard had stopped the pack of them in mid blitz.

They offered him their leftover change from last night's dinner to get the quiz answers without having to actually view the exhibits. He probably thought it was in the best interests of the museum to keep these barbarians as far from Grecian urns and fragile porcelains as possible. They had drawn caricatures of us as their favorite mummies. Foiled again, we paid them off and unleashed all but the youngest on the streets of London and their beloved Pizza Hut. They returned late that afternoon, having used the prize money to have their left ears pierced in Sloane Square.

The fathers, who were attending a convention, wisely gave us the next day off. They managed to get the front paws to the zoo, but the errant hindquarters, who had promised to be at Buckingham Palace for the Changing of the Guard, never showed.

the Natter Rivers with a gillie who lectured them without interruption on the history of fly-fishing. Elizabeth and I paid homage to Jane Austen, who is buried in Winchester Cathedral, and heard boys' choir practice in the cathedral at Salisbury. Her portion of the beast toured Stonehenge; mine ate yet another ham-and-cheese sandwich at the Superette in Heathfield. Bodiam Castle, where we stopped for tea, was a hit because it has almost no historical significance and the keepers allowed our children to climb all over it without having to sit still for the twelve-minute video on thirteenth-century castle life.

At Sissinghurst in Kent, the lovely gardens and home of Vita Sackville-West and Harold Nicholson, I could have stayed all day, but my eldest son hurled some sort of stick off the tower, nearly spearing an innocent tourist, and we were asked to leave.

When the beast proclaimed the hamburgers at Heathrow Airport the best part of the trip, Elizabeth and I kissed it good-bye, handed the choke chain to the fathers, and hopped the next British Caledonia flight to Paris.

A decade earlier, when my children were very small, I read a novel by Alison Lurie in which the main character, Erica, described her teenage children as "awful lodgers who pay no rent, whose leases cannot be terminated." During the beastly summer of '85, I thought Erica's summation was just right.

Hoofhearted

◆

I didn't want to write about this, because my intent is to lead the subject into a closet and seal the door shut forever. But ignoring it is not working. By writing about it, however, I run the risk of raising the topic for more public discussion and, worse, of labeling myself forever as that woman who wrote about . . . well, my favorite editor says we can call it flatulence.

Me and Chaucer. Remember how shocking it was to read beyond the "Whan that Aprille" prologue that we all memorized in high school to these lines in *The Miller's Tale:*

'Spek, swete brid, I noot nat wher thou art.'
This Nicholas anon leet flee a fart,
As greet as it had been a thonderdent [thunderbolt],
That with the strook he was almost yblent [blinded].

I wonder if the passage would even provoke a smirk among students today. That particular F-word is now so ubiquitous that the humor of a classic *Saturday Night Live* sketch relied on the actor's surprising the audience by *not* saying it. Senior citizens sporting T-shirts inscribed with "Old Fart" and "Old Fart's Wife" stroll the malls hand in hand. On Central Expressway I once saw a billboard that assaulted drivers with CALL 976-FART. My three sons tripped over each other racing into the house to place the call, which they later said was just some guy making noises and talking about picking his nose.

When he was a fourth grader, I took my youngest son shopping for a birthday present for a school friend in a novelty shop near our local university. I should have turned on my heel when I saw the boxer shorts bearing the message "There's a party in my pants, and you're invited." Everything my son deemed acceptable as a gift was grossly vulgar. We had a choice, it seemed, of fake snot, a small bust of someone named Phineas Phart, some farting powder, and a T-shirt with a hole burned in the front and "Who farted?" printed across the back. Over William's protest, I bought his friend a nice sports thermos.

I have observed for several years that little boys in car pools hit the window buttons and loudly demand to know "Who farted?" as if I were not present. "It's in the dictionary," one of my sons said in their defense when I threatened to dump them out on the curb. They collapsed in giggling fits when my son recited the definition from my old college dictionary— "an explosion of gas between the legs." It was the second word my sons taught the French exchange student who lived with us one summer. On a rare getaway to New York with my husband several years ago, I cried in the opening scene of Neil Simon's Broadway hit *Biloxi Blues* while the rest of the audience split their sides. I had not come all the way from Texas to watch teenage boys torch one another's behinds.

My sons tell me that deliberately breaking wind in school

is as common as throwing spit wads was in my day. "Oh, yeah, you should have been in my chemistry class after lunch," one said. "Somebody was always cranking one out and muttering, 'Speak to me, sloppy joe.' People get sent to the office all the time for it." I can remember the embarrassment of being summoned to a preschool to fetch a son who would not refrain from biting other children. That pales in comparison with the possibility of a conference with the high school vice principal over this infraction.

William claims that even girls are getting into the noisy act. I'm speechless! Please, girls, this is not an equal-rights issue! Have we lost all sense of decorum? When the quietest girl in my senior English class emitted an unmistakable squeaker during an exam and compounded her misery by saying in a tiny voice, "S'cuse me," the entire class reddened and stared straight at their papers, and the incident, though unforgettable, was never mentioned. That anybody would do such a thing on purpose would have been unthinkable.

I'm inclined to blame Chaucer. The Roman satirist Petronius thought it was pretty funny too, but he didn't speak English. My less literate sons blame everything on my "stupid sixties generation" and its liberated vocabulary. They suggest that I cool off by writing a letter to Mel Brooks, whose 1974 movie *Blazing Saddles,* with its scene of cowboys noisily eating beans around the campfire, put this kind of humor in the public domain.

Despite my Puritan name, maintaining a look of constant disapproval does not come naturally to me. I grew up listening to the locker-room vulgarity of my teenage older brother, whom I adored. When I was learning to read, adults in my family thought it great sport to spell out the letters h-o-o-f-h-e-a-r-t-e-d for me to pronounce. And deep in my heart, I believe that a family without a whoopee cushion ordered from the back of *Boys' Life* magazine to put in the chair of some unsuspecting grandmother at Thanksgiving probably lacks the humor to weather the vicissitudes of life. It's just that what was intended for occasional sophomoric knee-slapping hilarity *en famille* has become so public that it is making me sick.

My sons are embarrassed that I've written this. They should be.

Foreign Influences

◆

Import

Nicolas was blond and very blue-eyed and fourteen. Picture Leonardo DiCaprio. (My boys said "Ivan Drago.") Jack was fifteen; Drew, thirteen; and William, a precocious nine. I needed another teenager in my house that summer like a hole in the head, but this one spoke French. Like Calvin Trillin, I too speak French—nouns. Actually I know a few present and *passé composé* verbs as well. I must have believed that having this young Parisian friend of a friend in our home for the summer would recharge my own language-learning ambitions and provide much-needed European enrichment for the three motorcycle-crazed philistines I was rearing.

My family was not nearly as enthusiastic about this undertaking as I was. Having a guest for two months would put a strain on most households. Very casual families like ours, with a high degree of intimacy and uncivilized habits, have a hard time cleaning up their act for visitors. Would he be horrified at unclosed bathroom doors and underwear parades? How would I explain the bizarre attack-and-chase game my boys play in which the youngest brother ends up with no pants on at the dinner table? Who would assure him that all American families were not like us?

When we met him at the airport, I bravely tried my French in introducing Nicolas to my family. It was immediately apparent that I had never mastered the familiar pronoun and verb forms that one uses with a child. Who ever anticipates any familiarity with the French?

Riding home from the airport, my boys began the important interrogation. They flipped the radio dial through various rock stations. Nicolas smiled in recognition. "Tears for Fears," he said, causing my boys to applaud and give him the thumbs-up. "Duran, Duran," he grinned. Then he spoke his first English sentence: "Michael Jackson, he ees finish." Awright! The Frenchman had passed their cultural awareness test.

That only made him minimally acceptable. He scored more points on arrival at our house by immediately supplying them with the French words for "fart" and "queer." First things first. His presence, however, gradually elicited the oddest behavior in my sons. How could I have been so conscious of sibling rivalry each time I brought a new baby home from the hospital and yet have failed to anticipate the impact of this four-teen-year-old French import?

Why wouldn't they be jealous of him? He was a movie-star-handsome teenager without a single pimple, and he spoke an exotic language that visibly enchanted their mother. His book bag of summer reading, an idea dear to their mother's heart, was full of the works of French philosophers, which he had to comprehend by September or fall perilously behind in his Baccalaureat preparation. Nic was the son of a Parisian chef, and he took great interest in dinner preparation, slicing mushrooms and tomatoes like a pro, artfully composing salads the likes of which this family had never seen. Accustomed to long, civilized French meals, he lingered at our dinner table talking with John and me while my own sons tapped their fingers and feet, impatient to bolt. He kissed us good night on both cheeks, as all good French children do.

He was also a remarkable athlete, which did nothing to endear him to my competitive three. "I am zee beeg best," he immodestly announced. I had to search out new tennis partners in the neighborhood for him when my own sons proved no competition at all. My husband gloated for days when he finally trounced the cocky young Agassi on the court.

To expend some of the energy that builds to dangerous levels in boys when the swimming pool is closed and it's too hot to be outside, I took all four boys ice skating at the local mall. My boys, having lived in Texas all their lives, had only attempted this sport at a birthday party or two. With wobbly ankles, they awkwardly gripped the side rails while Monsieur Silver Skates sailed around the rink like an Olympian. Unable to take out their frustration and humiliation on our guest, they took their hands off the rail to vent their anger on one other. Jack fell first, Drew laughed, Jack whacked him hard, Drew choked back tears, then tripped William, who fell on Jack, who had just righted himself. They shoved, kicked, and were finally asked to leave the rink when they landed on the ice in a pile that obstructed the other skaters. They glumly pulled off their skates and sat sulking beside me while Saint Nicolas was recruited for a local teen ice hockey team.

To all of this, add the fact that the mother of this household was acting more like a smitten teenager than the directress of a cultural exchange. In my eagerness to embrace his language and to improve my own pronunciation, Nicolas and I quickly established an easy rapport, with inside jokes that rankled my own boys. The Froggie could do no wrong. If he bruised his toe at the swimming pool, I rendered solicitous first aid. Simone Beck and Julia Child were resurrected in my kitchen. Baguettes and chevre and huge bowls of fruit replaced the usual cache of chips, salsa, and Snickers.

At the video store he selected *An Officer and a Gentleman,* a movie I deemed a little sexy for my own guys. "My mother, she would not worry about the sex. It is a part of life, yes? She would never want me to see the violence you allow your sons to watch." My boys did a slow burn that summer as Arnold Schwarzenegger and Bruce Willis were edged out by Richard Gere and Humphrey Bogart (*Encore, une fois,* Sam).

That same summer a friend of mine in San Antonio was similarly housing a couple of Swedish pentathletes. We compared notes on our reactions to the European Adonises under our roofs. Becky admitted that she was up at dawn putting on eyeliner before breakfast. I was squeezing fresh orange juice, running to the French bakery to get the freshest croissants, and taxing my rudimentary French by reading two-day-old copies of *Le Monde* and *Figaro* at the bookstore to shore up what I thought to be the embarrassingly provincial conversation that my family produced at dinner. Nicolas said he could not understand my husband's English at all. "I theenk he speaks comme un cowboy, John Wayne." "John Wayne" did not find this remark sufficient incentive to improve his enunciation.

My sons called Nicolas "Froggie snail eater." They watched him carefully, eager to bring to my attention any fault they perceived. William refused to leave him alone with our dog, the only creature in our house with whom he had no language barrier. "Why are you so worried about Nic with Rosie? See, he pets her just the way you do. He has a Siberian husky of his own in France." "Mom, don't you know? They eat dogs in France. He's probably just looking for her juiciest parts."

Well instructed by his mother, Nicolas dutifully hung up

his clothes while my slobs began the summer ritual of dropping theirs on the floor. Unaccustomed to the constant laundering that goes on in American homes, this young man frugally wore his shirts and shorts several times before putting them in the laundry basket I had provided. I found it endearing. My sons, of course, thought it was disgusting. So French. Phew!

They made fun of his clothes. He wore an unconstructed sport coat, thin pink socks, and houndstooth-checked pants when we dressed for church. He buttoned his sport shirts to the neck. My boys were still wearing what they called tidy whites, but Nic wore wild boxers dotted with lipstick prints, naked ladies jumping out of cakes, and checklists of French girls' names with a few already checked off. And he wore them all with the confidence of a Parisian, even at fourteen.

I scanned the postcards he lovingly wrote to his "*trés chère maman*" before I mailed them for him as if they were my report cards. My classroom French was useless in this translation effort, since he, of course, used colloquial slang with his parents. "La bouffe n'est pas si mauvaise." My formal dictionary translated *bouffe* as "musical comedy." Was he commenting on my singing in the kitchen? No, a French friend assured me, he was assessing the food. Oh, so my *boeuf en daube* was not so bad. When he used the word "super" in his correspondence, I never knew whether he was inserting an English word (in which case we were succeeding) or employing the French word *super,* which means "to suck."

The summer was not constant animosity. Despite all of my wrongheaded efforts, the boys gradually connected with Nicolas on their own terms. They played hard together every day. We went to Six Flags, to water amusement parks, to the local swimming pool, where Nicolas learned to play Marco Polo and Gutter Ball, and of course, to the Mesquite Championship Rodeo, where he bought a straw cowboy hat. I stifled my impulse to remark that not since Paul Newman in *Hud* had a Western hat been so enhanced. Keeping my adoring comments to myself gradually allowed my sons to reach a certain rapprochement with "Zee Beeg Best." When they disagreed about chess rules, however, mine gave no quarter. Nicolas would protest, "Een my country . . . ," and the three Americans would respond, "This isn't your country, Zulu. We're playing American style." Some afternoons I would find them all asleep on the floor, my four beautiful sunburned boys with chlorine-streaked hair, completely exhausted by the incessant competition, a much-contested board game overturned beside them.

The neighbors were charmed by this French addition to our household. Drew remarked, "Having a French guy at your house could get to be a fad around here." Nicolas's English improved a bit. He read children's books aloud to William, and I read Agatha Christie novels in French to him. Neither of us followed our respective story lines with much ease, but we corrected each other's pronunciation.

We took field trips to Austin and San Antonio in my Peugeot station wagon, with the beeps of their video games in the backseat driving me nuts. Picnicking on the grounds of the state capitol, my eldest grumbled sarcastically, "Don't you just love Mother's little cultural adventures? We get Evian water and turkey on baguette instead of Dr Peppers and cheeseburgers." They spotted Pizza Inn billboards and delighted me by singing out *en français*, "Pour Pizza dehors, c'est Pizza dedans" (For pizza out, it's Pizza Inn). The River Walk in San Antonio was the closest I could come to Paris, and despite the hundred-plus temperature, Nicolas pronounced it "super." Communicating the significance of the Alamo was beyond my French. "I don't understahn what ees this Alamo," he said.

We reluctantly rented the John Wayne video for him when we got home.

Needing a break from my job as cultural exchange activity director one day, I sent the four boys downtown to have lunch with my husband at the Dallas Club, an establishment that at the time prohibited women in the main dining room. I loved it that Nicolas found this American phenomenon so preposterous. "No French man," he said, "would ever want to sit at a table without women."

One evening he didn't go outside with the rest of the neighborhood kids after dinner. Drew said, "I think he's crying, Mom . . . or maybe he's just jammin' out with his Walkman." "He's probably just had it with us," I said. "How long can anyone maintain such a superficial existence, speaking in the present tense about concrete things with a bunch of half-civilized Texans?" What would his French mother think when he told her about the lardy Mexican food we ate with such relish once a week? Would he tell her that we watched with fiendish delight as he downed his first jalapeño pepper, believing it to be a zucchini? I knew from the effusive letters from his mother that he left lying around the house that he was a much-adored child. That summer I not only wanted to speak French, I wanted to become a French mother who closes her letter to her son with "Tout le monde ici t'embrasse (Everyone here embraces you)." "Athélia te lêche, Léon te câline et mois, je te couvre de baiser mon petit chéri que j'aime (Athelia [his dog] licks you. Leon [the cat] caresses you, and I cover you with kisses, my dear little one whom I love."

The cultural exchange drew to a close in August, all too soon for me, perhaps not soon enough for the rest of my household. From my boys, Nicolas had learned to announce that things that pleased him were "cool," although with his accent, it came out "kule." Besides many more trips to amusement parks than I ordinarily agreed to, did my children see any benefit in this summer experience? At dinner after taking Nic to the airport for his return to France, laden with Texas sports equipment for his friends Olivier and Roman and an antique American quilt for his mother, I quizzed my own three. They acknowledged that they could still sing the Pizza Inn commercial in French. They also knew the French word for "leech" after watching Humphrey Bogart/Katharine Hepburn in *African Queen* and hearing Nic yell, *"Les sangsues, les sangsues."* Sensing that I had hoped for more, they launched into the mimicking routine that I had squelched all summer. "Pahs zee butter, Muzzer," said William. "I am wait with great impatience," Drew added. "My bruzzer, he ees too *faineant,* lazy," Jack offered. All was not lost. They had learned to speak pidgin English with a French accent.

Thenk hevvin for leetle boys . . .

Export

The following summer the roles were reversed. My middle son, Drew, only thirteen years old, became the little prince of Nicolas's household in Paris and at their country home in Normandy. Knowing that he would be going to France in late June, and knowing firsthand the difficulties that Nicolas had experienced navigating in English, Drew still made no attempt to learn any French. I gave him an absurdly basic book called *French in Ten Minutes a Day*; I taped French words on objects all over the house; Drew ignored the book and consistently averted his eyes from my labels, especially the word *douche* pasted in the shower.

Nicolas had arrived in the United States the previous year unescorted, but Drew was a year younger. I couldn't see a thirteen-year-old, especially one whose French vocabulary consisted of a pizza jingle and the word for leeches, managing the potential disasters of international travel alone. Besides, I was eager for more time in Paris myself.

Recent Libyan terrorism had reduced the average U.S. tourist's interest in European travel that summer, so my son and I had whole banks of coach-class seats to stretch out on. He beat me in a few hands of gin rummy and then tapped out as if our disembarkment the next morning would bring nothing more extraordinary than Saturday cartoons.

We were welcomed at Orly Airport by Brigitte, Nicolas's mother; Nicolas; his younger brother, Julien; the boys' grandfather Jean-Claude; and Diane, the friend of a friend who had brought about the whole exchange. Two small French cars were required to transport all of us and our baggage, so I joined the two women while Drew piled in with Nic, Julien, and Grandpère.

We reconnected at a small French restaurant on Mont-martre called L'Assommoir. (Nic had perhaps remembered my struggling to read Zola's novel by the same name the previous summer.) A bit jet-lagged and euphoric, I felt as if I were in a French film. Jean-Claude, the grandfather, was Maurice Chevalier with an endless repertoire of jokes for me, which he told with enough body language and gesturing to surmount our language barrier. When the wine was brought, we toasted our safe arrival. Jean-Claude clinked his glass against mine and said, "You know why we do thees. Wine, eet brings pleasure to the eyes, the nose, the taste, all the senses except the ears. We 'clink-clink' our glasses like thees so we can hear it as well."

"Ah, oui . . . bien sur."

Drew sat sullenly watching me. I shot him a poison dart when he ordered a Coca-Cola. When he was told they had no Cokes, his new French mother suggested he might try a refreshing *menthe d'eau* (mint water?). Back at our modest hotel room, made luxurious by four dozen fragrant roses sent by Drew's new family, I called home to recount the pleasures of our first encounter: *"Sandre grillée en sauce vierge,* and *le grandpère, trés charmant."* Drew said, "Be sure to tell them that you have brought me to a country where they think Scope is a good substitute for Coke!"

His willingness to take on this exchange was beginning to go sour, and I could now understand how much easier the transition would have been if I hadn't accompanied him. I suggested we both take a nap. Upon awakening, he looked at me a little wildly and said, "Oh, no, we're still here. I thought maybe it was a nightmare. I have to go home. These people expect me to speak French. Even Nic has forgotten his English. I haven't understood one word since we got here." A few moments later, he hit his head on the poorly designed shower, which gave him a good excuse to scream.

Whatever the following day brought, it would no doubt be an improvement. I sensed that the quicker I receded from this picture, the better. Brigitte and I agreed that Drew should spend the second night at the family's apartment and I would move to a small hotel by myself on the Left Bank.

After a full night's sleep, we did feel better. Brigitte felt compelled to show Drew the routine sights of Paris, so we herded the three boys up and down the Eiffel Tower and on *bateaux mouches* on the Seine. The heat was uncharacteristically oppressive, and the boys were more interested in the topless sunbathers along the banks than the flying buttresses of Notre Dame. We dined that night at Le Persil Fleur, the family's restaurant, very near the old Paris Opera. I admired from the opposite end of the table my little prince, who was beginning to find his way with this most hospitable family and their friends, who were celebrating their daughter's ninth birthday. I deliberately did not make eye contact with him when the appetizer, raw salmon, was served. I did catch his flicker of disappointment when the much-heralded birthday cake for Eleanor turned out to be a concoction of sorbet and fruit. Without so much as drumming his fingers, however, he successfully endured a dinner that began at 9:00 P.M. and lasted three hours.

I returned to my hotel alone, swallowing my concerns about how he might starve in the midst of culinary delicacies so relished by French children. Would the ubiquitous cigarette smoke irritate his allergies? How would he manage with so few French phrases? He seemed so young, so American, so innocent among these Parisian children. Was I wrong to impose on him the desires and ambitions of my own heart?

My worries were largely unfounded. By the time we met up the next day, he seemed to have settled into a new life in the Seventeenth Arrondissement. He had played tennis with Nicolas's friends and watched enough French television to conclude, "Mom, the French just don't take anything too seriously." If I had worried that family life at my house was too casual, Drew assured me that Brigitte was in the middle of some kind of remodeling of the apartment and until the fabric for the walls arrived, she was permitting the boys to mark their heights on the wall and draw funny cartoons, mostly involving Maria, the Portuguese maid. He had watched some quiz program on French television called *Sexy Follies,* which required contestants to remove an article of clothing each time they missed an answer. "There are naked people on TV all the time," he said with obvious delight. Drew especially liked the fact that Nicolas's Siberian husky, Athelia, entered and exited the apartment through an open window on the ground floor. At lunch that day, my boy seemed as animated as the rest of this exuberant extended family as they made plans to leave for their summer home on the Normandy coast the next day. Brigitte would drive the car, crammed with all things necessary to open the house, and the children would travel independently by train.

At Brigitte's suggestion, Drew spent the last night in Paris with me. I treated him to a beefsteak and french fries for dinner and let him have both croissants the next morning for breakfast. We rendezvoused with Nicolas, Julien, and one of their friends at the family's restaurant for the departure to the train station that would take them to the tiny village of Portbail on the coast. I had romantic notions about waving my son off from the train platform, an appropriate end to this French film we seemed to be making.

The boys piled into the taxi, and when I squeezed in with them, the beady-eyed cabdriver erupted with all of the French gesturing. "Non, non, non, madame, seulement quatre personnes." They were running late for the train, so I hugged and kissed my boy hard, and hopped out of the cab. "Don't look back at me now, Mom," he said as I closed the taxi door. "I'm going to be awfully homesick." Eyes stinging, I touched fingers to lips, tossed the last kiss over my shoulder, and disappeared into the bustle of the Metro.

I have only the sketchiest knowledge of his life in the French countryside. He wrote a couple of postcards. I know that Brigitte kept him very busy and perhaps indulged him much as I had done Nicolas at our house. She also pushed him in ways that I admired. With none of the prerequisites, he joined her boys in advanced sailing classes on the cold and rocky Normandy coast. What terror this child who had never known port from starboard must have overcome with waves crashing all around and instructors yelling at him in French! Brigitte admitted that he appeared so chilled and stunned after the first day that she drew him a bubble bath and allowed him to soak until dinner, using all of the hot water the rural French plumbing could muster. Much like the sailing, he negotiated village dances with no more French than "Je suis Americain" and a few *oui*'s and *non*'s ventured in response to questions he didn't understand. He had more success with horseback-riding lessons, fireworks on the beach, Ping-Pong, and the enchanting *char à voile*. The winds on the beach were apparently strong enough to propel a sand chariot, a wheeled contraption with large adjustable sail, at great speed down the shore.

Meals were a problem. What a perplexing dilemma for a family whose living was made by serving up some of the finest food in Paris. Portbail had no McDonald's, and bloody rare beef, duck liver, brains, kidneys, and the various organ meats so commonplace in the French kitchen would not pass the lips of this peanut butter American kid. Poor Brigitte tried to make a spaghetti dish employing real American catsup, but with no success. He even bypassed the spectacular desserts, tarts, and *dacquoises* prepared as special treats by the grandmother Jeannine. Brigitte feared he would return home with nutritional deficiencies, since he spent most of his allowance at the local candy store.

Still, his French mother wrote of him with great affection. "Drew est un amour. C'est un garçon plein de charme, trés vif et vraiment trés sympathique (Drew is a love. He is a boy full of charm, very lively, and truly very pleasant)," and for that I was relieved. If there were jealousies or rivalrous feelings from her own boys, she never mentioned it.

His departure from France was not without incident. After he bade adieu to his French family and entered the "passengers only" area of the airport, an airline strike required even more resourcefulness on his part. He wisely befriended Air France flight attendants by engaging them in gin rummy to pass the time during the lengthening delay. They apparently expedited his transfer to another airline, and he emerged from what was surely an exhausting return home with a radiance and a cheerfulness I'd rarely seen.

The parent who meets the child's plane gets what I call the first imprint, the initial, effusive spilling of details that will never be told again. It is a brief window on their lives that snaps shut all too soon. A thirteen-year-old cannot assess the value of such an adventure. And it is presumptuous of any parent to do it for them.

Did he learn to speak French? No. He does speak Spanish however, with considerable facility, and perhaps this French foray in some way fueled his confidence to go to school and work in Mexico during his college years. On the other hand, it could have just been the frigid University of Michigan weather. Did he establish a bond with a French family that he will treasure the rest of his life? Probably not, but I did. I am the female in the family, the one who connects, who writes the letters, supplies yearly photos, and remembers to send small Christmas gifts.

Twelve years later, the invitation to the wedding of Nicolas and Nathalie, to be held in Finisterre (literally, the end of the earth) arrived. Guess who went, who drank fine champagne, who ate fresh oysters from the Brittany coast, and who danced for the sheer joy of it with Grandpère Jean-Claude at the reception until 4 A.M.? I did. And Baby Augustin, who appeared the following year, will know that he has an American grandmother, too.

The things our kids do for us.

Fifteen Sucks

◆

April 29, _____
R. R_____
Head of Upper School

Dear Ms. R_____:

My ninth grader and I have an appointment to discuss his high school plan with you next week. Don't expect much excitement or enthusiasm on his part.

You must know that fifteen, at least for boys, is surely the worst time to discuss the future. Fifteen still thinks it's funny to fart in class. Fifteen responds to life with two phrases: "bull" and "no way." Fifteen brings salad dressing in a jar for his submarine sandwich and announces to his buddies at lunch that it's his aborted little sister. Fifteen would watch endless reruns of G.I. Joe cartoons. Fifteen begs for guitar lessons and then begs to quit when he realizes that the teacher actually expects him to learn to read music. Fifteen gets an ear pierced at the mall out of utter boredom and then gets demerits for it in history class when Mr. K decides to use his head to demonstrate the trajectory of the bullet that killed Lincoln. Fifteen likes girls and makes baroque plans to see them on the weekend, but the plans never quite pan out. Fifteen can't drive. Fifteen sucks.

If my son were honest about his goal for the year, I do believe he would say it was to grow more armpit hair under his left arm before basketball season. Our family has a history of late and lopsided puberty.

He currently regards the next three academic years with dread. School has never held any appeal for him. When I awakened him for the second day of first grade, he looked stricken and said, "You mean I have to go again? I did that yesterday."

I don't fault his teachers. Some people are simply not blessed with intellectual curiosity at fifteen—or perhaps it gets stifled when you have brothers who, despite their mother's protests, use you as a straight man. I probably started it that rainy afternoon during his babyhood when I let them paint Groucho eyebrows on him. Or perhaps it is the Irish streak from my side of the family. We cannot resist the impulse to see life in a comic light. It seems to preclude high achievement.

On the other hand, this is a very pleasant kid. When he does speak, he doesn't resort to "ya know" or "I was, like . . ." He's insightful. He's funny if you are amused by such speculation as "What if your head and your butt traded places?" He seems to have good judgment about people. He's a loyal friend. He's a little shy and believes the best policy is to keep bottom lip firmly pressed against upper lip rather than risk saying something foolish. He's well organized. If the school gave a prize for cleanest locker, he'd win—probably because he has no science notes.

Please assure the college counselor that I have had some experience in crafting sow's ears into silk purses for college admissions offices.

I am providing this background material to you now because I will be mute during our meeting on Wednesday. Fifteen believes that the best mother is one who never misses an opportunity to shut up.

Sincerely yours,

First Job

◆

"First to the car," nine-year-old William yelled at Jack over his shoulder as his fingers touched our scorching black station wagon. "First in the backseat," he continued as he fumbled with the snarled seat belt. "First to get my seat belt fastened," he announced triumphantly, bouncing as Jack and I waited for some of the Texas heat to escape the ovenlike interior. "First not to care," said Jack, as he slid calmly in beside the crestfallen and bewildered little brother.

The sixteenth summer brought this eldest son, Jack, his first real job, with a time clock, a supervisor, a uniform, and a generous weekly paycheck. Previously, he had mowed yards, thrown newspapers, and baby-sat long hours to secure a bit of financial independence, but this real job set him apart from his brothers and us and from the world of his childhood.

Jack's abrupt retirement from what I call the jackass competition with his brothers had a unsettling effect. Suddenly he was no longer a part of the spotlight hide-and-seek games that made our house with its wraparound porch and big trees the summer gathering place for neighborhood kids. He was once the commander of the water balloon campaigns that consumed long summer days. He organized the forces and masterminded the storage and strategic placement of Igloo coolers brimming with water bomb ammunition. At sixteen, he couldn't even be lured into a sock fight, the indoor version of water balloon war, which similarly vented male aggression at my house without inflicting serious bodily harm.

He put away those childish things. His voice changed that year. At least I think it did. Phone solicitors quit asking him if he was the "lady of the house." Our communication that sixteenth year was limited to my filling the air around his two-word responses. When I probed for more, he responded with the exasperating phrase "Don't worry about it, Mom."

He got his driver's license that year, and, as I discovered when I accidentally laundered his wallet, a fake ID. The face on that laminated illegal license looked only a little older than the face on another card that I fished out of the same damp wallet—a Padre Island go-cart license. I wondered if in a tense moment, he might display the wrong card.

"For your mother's sake, couldn't you at least have made your birth legitimate?" I asked when I confronted him with the contraband ID. The phony license made him a resident of Durant, Oklahoma, and dated his birth in May of 1966, about a month before his dad and I were married. It's hard for a parent to fathom what status is conferred when a teenager assumes the identity of a twenty-one-year-old bastard Okie.

This summer job working in a warehouse, however, threatened to age Jack more than his Oklahoma driver's license. His janitorial duties, euphemistically called "damage control," began at 6 A.M. each day. Left undisturbed in his bed, this son could easily have slept away the remainder of his adolescence. I had to admire his determination as he set his alarm for 5:15 that first night as well as his optimism about the punctuality of another teenager who provided his transportation to work most mornings. He was determined that this job would be none of my business, and for the most part he succeeded. He concocted a protein powder breakfast drink that could be prepared in the blender and consumed in short order, so I wouldn't worry about his breakfast. He packed lunches so he wouldn't be tempted to spend his hard-earned money eating lunch in fast-food restaurants. When he slept through his alarm once or twice, he was so contrite about my having to get up and drive him to work that the next time he called a taxi and paid for it from his own paycheck.

This sixteenth summer was not at all what my friends had predicted. I lost no sleep waiting up late at night for my teenage son with the new driver's license. Jack was so exhausted by his job that if he wasn't at work, he was in his bed asleep. My own body rhythms reverted to those of a new mother. I shushed his little brother's noisy spotlight games in the yard after 9 P.M. because Jack had to get his sleep; I awoke intermittently during the night to wonder if he'd set his alarm, packed his lunch, and reconfirmed his car pool. Though he needed no 5 A.M. feeding, I woke up promptly with his alarm each morning and listened until I heard the car door slam. While the two half-awake teenagers drove through darkened streets toward the warehouse near Harry Hines Boulevard, I made my coffee and listened for sirens.

I'm not sure what I expected from this job. Jack expected money. Our incomes and consciences could never keep pace with this son's desire for luxury items—stereo components, stylish and peculiar French imported clothing, and pizzas delivered at odd hours of the day. I envisioned his paychecks going straight to the bank, earmarked for a car that he might be able to purchase before he went to college. Jack had other ideas.

Without consulting me, he arranged to receive his weekly pay in cash. I still have on my desk a grinning photograph of him in his sweat-stained uniform, with a fan of twenty dollar bills spread across his chest. As the weeks passed and the cash stack grew higher, I explained once again the importance of keeping money in the bank, earning interest, and saving for a long-term goal like college or a car.

"I'm not saving for a car, Mom. I'll never have that much money. This money is going for new stereo speakers, or maybe a TV for my room," he said.

"Oh, no, it's not," I snapped. "You're putting at least half of that money in the bank. You've bought enough stereo equipment to open an electronics store, and nobody in this house is having a television set in his own room!"

"It's my money!" he yelled in a voice that brought his father into the room. "I'm the one who gets up at five, and I'm buying whatever I want with it."

"Don't you speak to your mother in that tone of voice," John barked. Things quickly escalated to tantrum levels on both sides. I found myself, as I often do, glancing over my shoulder in search of the real mother to take charge. Blindsided by this new declaration of independence, we grounded him. His job, of course, had already restricted his life beyond our punishment. He slammed and locked his bedroom door.

Two days later, just before his 9 P.M. bedtime, Jack came to our room, stared at his shoes, and mumbled, "Uh, this is really stupid and you're gonna kill me, but I need help. Sunday afternoon I was so mad at you that I gave all my money [$300] to Matt [his friend] to buy a television set for me. Well, he let the salesman at the appliance store talk him into buying a scarred-up floor model. I don't want that old used TV, but the sales ticket says "final payment/no returns" and they won't take it back and now they've got my three hundred dollars. Can you do something?"

I was simultaneously so embarrassed for him and yet so proud of his ability to swallow his pride and confess the fiasco that I couldn't even gloat. We agreed to negotiate with the appliance store only if he agreed that the retrieved money as well as a percentage of future earnings go straight to his savings account. He was in no position to argue.

During that summer, I observed that the things one learns from a summer job go far beyond the middle-class virtues of responsibility, punctuality, and respect for the dollar. Since most teenage boys' marketable skills run to digging, lifting, stacking, packing, sweeping, and crushing, they usually wind up working with men who are products of a more rough-and-tumble world, a world my suburban teenager hardly knew existed. While Jack used his weekly paycheck to bring him closer to possessing overpriced stereo speakers, his coworkers, whose lives sounded like country-and-western song lyrics, bought groceries and paid overdue rent with theirs. His new acquaintances invited him to neighborhoods he'd never seen before. "You'll know my house, man," said Gilberto. "I spray-paint my name across the front." Jack offered no reciprocal invitations. He had always thought our house not quite grand enough for his own friends. Now he was ashamed of our bounty.

The summer raised other questions. "How do the black guys understand me, but I can't understand them? Why does the boss's son come in late and leave early?" He met shirkers and hard workers of all races. He was highly honored and thoroughly entertained when invited on Friday afternoons to share the camaraderie at a picnic table next to the convenience store, where his coworkers broke out their weekend six-packs.

He learned about pawnshops and collection agencies and greedy sharks who charged six dollars to cash a hundred-dollar check. He observed, admired, and sympathized with the hardworking foremen whose diligence and loyalty to the company had secured jobs for their offspring, who then frequently blew the opportunities by showing up late, drunk, or not at all.

By midsummer, he had developed pride not only in his earning capacity but in his ability to make his way in this blue-collar world.

One afternoon, when he was still in his dirt-smeared uniform and heavy black shoes, I overheard him in the living room with his greatest fan, little brother William, flipping through the pages of a coffee table book of photographs taken of oil-field workers. "See, Willie, this is who I am," he said, pointing to a tattooed roughneck standing in front of his new automobile.

Periodically, he announced to Drew, who has always believed that the Publishers Clearing House Sweepstakes will save him from having to break a sweat, "I can tell that you are amounting to absolutely nothing! If I catch you or Willie hanging around this house mooching off Mom and Dad after your eighteenth birthday, I'll kick your butts out of here."

He looked on other less strenuously employed folks with similar disdain. In August, when we shopped for school clothes, he sized up the shoe clerk, then leaned over and whispered to me, "Do you think he makes more an hour than I do?" Watching other clerks standing around, he'd say, "I don't see how they can call this a job. They aren't doing anything." Waiters and fast-food workers, secretaries and file

clerks—anybody who got to work in air-conditioning all day—
got the same reverse snobbery.

Common wisdom suggests that backbreaking summer jobs
are useful in teaching upwardly mobile suburban kids the
value of higher education. I suppose that thought crossed
Jack's mind, but I think the lessons of his warehouse summers were far more complicated and valuable than that.

"Don't worry about it, Mom."

I'm not.

Pumpitude

◆

It's taken three trips through adolescence with three very different sons to understand one universal truth about males. Size matters. When a pediatrician suggested that boys only grow while they're sleeping, all three of my boys took to their beds for marathon sleep sessions. While all of them have now achieved a height they deem acceptable, all were physical late bloomers. When I explained to Jack, then a skinny freshman in high school, that I was only 4'11" when I entered high school and that their father finished growing after we married, he responded, "You knew this and you still had children?"

For years they seemed stuck in what the pediatrician called "Stage One puberty." In those days, we speculated that our pediatrician's Stage Two required a five o'clock shadow and an out-of-wedlock child. At Back to School Night at the middle school, the coach hinted at the gruesome peer pressure of early adolescence by facetiously asking, "Do you let these guys take showers in their underwear at home?" Girls simply have no experience comparable to the daily humiliation of short, skinny boys with hairless armpits in a high school gym class shower.

This is the story of how Arnold Schwarzenegger, Joe Weider, a family of wrestlers called the Von Erichs, and pumpitude invaded my household and I learned to love them.

I suppose there were males in my own youth who sent off for Charles Atlas bodybuilding courses advertised in the back of comic books, but they never mentioned it to me. While we were not immune to the charms of lifeguards and football players, our matinee idols were Cary Grant and Gregory Peck, men who did not walk like apes or wear tank tops. Of course, we did have Marlon Brando, but look how he turned out. I do not think women of my generation ever commented on the "pecs, lats, buns, or biceps" of prospective dates. Gyms were sleazy places where guys with tattoos and Harleys hung out. I was not predisposed to enthusiastically embrace the fitness phenomenon of the late seventies and eighties.

"Chicks expect it now," one son said. "Didn't you ever want to date anyone who was 'ripped,' Mom?" They have relegated their relatively slim and reasonably fit dad to the *"Saturday Night Live* Hans and Franz girly man" category.

Jack, the eldest, began pumping iron while away in boarding school. He claimed it relieved boredom and gave him a sense of achievement that required study hall never did. Lifting weights seemed narcissistic to me, and I'm sure I expressed my regret that he'd chosen to pursue something so solitary over a team sport. What were these muscles for?

By the time he came home for summer vacation, he had transformed the standard Mackintosh skinny body into something I'm sure the Creator never intended. His neck had almost disappeared, and his chest muscles and bulging biceps required a larger shirt size. He entertained his younger brothers and startled me by spreading his *latissimus dorsi* muscles like a hooded cobra. I didn't get it. I blamed the Von Erichs, a wrestling family on television that my children tuned in to watch as soon as we got home from church each Sunday. It was as if my boys needed an immediate violent, vulgar antidote to the peaceful religious influences of the previous hour while they peeled off their Sunday clothes. World Championship Wrestling presented good versus evil wrestling in campy costumes.

I watched in horror as two of my sons blew their allowances on products from fitness magnate Joe Weider's array of gimmicks. The sport required weight belts, leg wraps, special gloves, and many visits to the health food store. My friends with daughters who seem to border on anorexia most of the time find it inconceivable that boys the same age consume high-calorie milk shakes made with a Weider protein powder called "Huge" or "Big." I'm saving a can or two with Joe Weider's big yellow mustachioed face on the front. When middle-aged spread hits these guys, I think they'll rue the day they choked down thousand-calorie concoctions.

Jack's diet, apart from the Weider powder, revolutionized my kitchen and shamed his Oreo-eating brothers. He ate only fish and chicken, pasta, leafy greens, fruit, and that horrible health-food peanut butter that wouldn't stay mixed. He ate his sandwiches dry, with no mayonnaise, and his toast was never buttered. He is probably the only teenager in history who ate no hamburgers in high school.

The earliest days of this fitness obsession worried me enough to see a counselor. I was prepared to tell the counselor that my bright and witty kid had suddenly abandoned all academic achievement and started on a track that seemed to lead only to World Championship Wrestling or Mr. Olympia contests. The bearded psychologist leaned back in his chair, smiled, and asked, "What's he bench-pressing these days?" I had no idea. I wasn't even sure what a bench press was.

"This is the most important thing in this kid's life right now, and you don't even know the level of his achievement?" the wise counselor asked. He went on to say that he'd taken up weights himself and found it an excellent way to relieve stress. "Maybe I'll see your son at the gym sometime. While most kids are drinking themselves into oblivion, sounds like you've got an extraordinarily healthy sixteen-year-old on your hands. I'd like to meet him."

For Christmas that year I capitulated and bought the boys a cheap weight set at a discount store. It was too little, too late, as usual. Jack's summer work money now financed his membership in the downtown YMCA, where the latest in free-weight equipment was all the rage. Drew tagged along with his more indulged friends to their posh health clubs or jumped from club to club on free introductory guest passes. Only the youngest, William, who had no "wheels," had to make do with the chinning bar on the closet door and "Mother's crummy weight set."

I warned them that adult life would never accommodate such foolishness. So much for my predictions about their adult lives. What gave me fits in their adolescence established disciplines that continue to keep them fit and healthy and relatively "ripped" in their twenty-something years. Cary Grant has left the building.

Driving Me Crazy

◆

"What is a hysterectomy?" the lanky fourteen-year-old demanded, slamming his book bag on the kitchen table and opening the refrigerator door.

Inured to such abrupt greetings and mildly pleased at the prospect of a substantive conversation with her teenage son, the mother launched into a full diagram of female plumbing, surgical technique, and hormone therapy. "Is that what you wanted to know?" she asked, noting his impatience with the length of her lecture.

"Nope, what I need to know is can *you* get one? Alan's mother had one last week, and he's getting a hardship driver's license Tuesday."

All three of my boys are licensed drivers, and I'm relieved that none of them required me to undergo surgery. There are, however, some hardships inherent in living with beginning drivers. And, as with a hysterectomy, there is a certain irrevocability—a no-going-back about the whole process.

My initial experiences with a driving child were gentle

enough. Jack, the firstborn, took his driver's education course while away at boarding school in Austin. He learned MoPac, Interstate 35, Loop 360, and Ben White Boulevard long before he knew Central Expressway or Stemmons Freeway in his own hometown, Dallas. He shaved the side mirror off a car backing out of the driveway, was ticketed for doing forty in a thirty on his way home from the dentist, was sideswiped and rear-ended by classmates at school, but because I never witnessed his learning to drive, never winced at his early uncertain lane changes, I have an unwarranted confidence in his driving ability.

With the second son, Drew, who turned sixteen earlier than most of his classmates, I quickly developed a callus on my right foot from pressing the phantom brakes on the passenger side. My sweaty hand clung to the handrail above the window, and even in the hottest days of summer, even in a linen blouse, I never failed to fasten my seat belt when I rode with him. He resented my alerting him to Stop signs and one-way streets, so I settled for sucking air through my teeth each time he ignored one or swiveled his head to the rear and abruptly changed lanes, leaving me powerless and alone to assess the changing traffic in front of us. A new driver's impulse is to swerve slightly away from the oncoming traffic, so I learned to steer empathetically with my stiffened body, leaning toward my young driver when the passenger side seemed destined to be shorn off by a truck driver dissatisfied with the reduced right lane space my son offered him.

I willingly left Central Expressway driving instruction to the foolhardy driver's ed instructor. When I venture onto that treacherous roadway, I choose the lane I need to be in immediately and do not cut in and out of traffic regardless of the pace. I have read stories about drivers' being armed, and I try not to antagonize anyone, especially those with bumper stickers that oppose gun control or read "Shit Happens."

After driving in Dallas for more than twenty years, I still consider each safe entrance made from the access road in my four-cylinder station wagon a divine dispensation. Deciding when to enter the flow of traffic and accelerating accordingly seem to require judgment and experience that I'm still acquiring. I lack the courage to accompany any sixteen-year-old on his first attempt.

I wasn't always such a coward. In my teenage years, when Texas was a more rural state, kids were licensed to drive at fourteen. I don't think that statute was enforced with any regularity in my hometown of Texarkana. Besides, unlaminated paper licenses without pictures were easily altered. My sixth-grade boyfriend had been driving a tractor and a truck on a farm since he was eight. By the time we were in the seventh grade (he was twelve), my parents allowed me to ride regularly with him in his brother's 1951 shiny red Ford with the courting knob. Well, he'd had four years of driving experience.

Driver's education is now mandatory in Texas for drivers under the age of eighteen. I'm glad. The newest drivers in my home are the last of the babies who lived dangerously. We wore no seat belts in their infancy, and I don't recall much restraint in their baby seats other than my swatting their legs every time they tried to climb out. They bounced along beside me in our '65 Chevrolet in unanchored graham cracker-encrusted baby seats that allowed them to see the world, baby seats designed to hurl them headfirst through the windshield in the event of an accident. Only my youngest son, born after the stiffer safety laws were enacted, has known a consistently cautious and buckled-up life. His older brothers frequently remind him, "William, childhood is not what it once was." Irrationally, I believe that their early experiences make them freer spirits behind the wheel and any caution that driver's education instilled is on the side of the angels.

The driving school that we selected for Drew cost almost as much as summer camp and didn't last as long. For one hour each evening for three and a half weeks, my son and a gaggle of other gangly fifteen-year-olds gathered in a hotel meeting room to be lectured on the rules of the road and to view the Department of Public Safety's films on collisions, which the boys dubbed "Crispy Critters." Besides the classroom instruction, they did seven cumulative hours of driving in nice automatic Buicks.

Judging from the catsup stains on my son's shirt and the milk shake cups he returned with each evening, I surmised that mastering a fast-food drive-through had replaced parallel parking on the driver's test. Dave, my son's driving instructor, was clearly more relaxed in the passenger seat than I was. Drew came home every night with new jokes that I could never have told or found amusing while taking a suburban corner at thirty miles an hour.

Nothing in the driver's ed curriculum, however, prepares a teenager for his first experience with government bureaucracy. Not one of the DPS stations is close to our house, and the address listed in the phone book for one that seemed closest led us to a vacant storefront. By the time we found the proper location, we had lost our early-morning advantage.

Driver's license bureaus have an Ellis Island quality about them. Citizenship is not a prerequisite for a license. I heard at least four foreign languages and a variety of American dialects while we inched forward toward the desk. Entire Oriental families were on hand to support a shy mother's reluctant foray onto the expressway of American life. Middle Eastern men hunkered and gestured on the sidewalk outside while they awaited their turn with the driving inspector. Hispanic babies dressed for the occasion in full Sunday garb patiently dozed in their strollers under the eyes of nervous mothers. Other restless children fought over potato chips and played "You can't git me . . ." until the young mother in tight jeans in front of me threatened, "Awright, Billy Earl, that's it. You don't git no school supplies." Only my son exuded confidence.

"Birth certificate?" said the weary clerk without looking up. I groaned audibly. Passing the buck and feigning ignorance, Drew turned to me and said, "Birth certificate, Mom?" This little adventure, begun as a birthday treat, had now eaten most of my morning. He had never mentioned needing a birth certificate. He turned quickly back to the clerk to avoid the killer laser I trained on him. "Uh, I brought my mom. She was there and can certify it," he said in his jocular manner that now failed him for the first time ever.

We made four trips in all to the license bureau, twice for the written test with and without proper documents and twice for the driving portion. I was comforted on one of those subsequent visits by the mother of a daughter returning for her eighth try. Maybe raising daughters isn't any easier, even if their insurance rates are lower. One woman told me that at one point while she was riding with her newly licensed daughter, parked cars loomed in their lane. "I was sure that she saw them," the mother said, "but less than a yard from the rear bumper of the parked car, I frantically grabbed the wheel to avoid the collision. 'What were you thinking?' I screamed at her. 'You won't believe this, Mom,' she said, 'but I just forgot that I was driving.'" While Drew was taking the driving test the first time, I heard enough similar tales to make me think insurance companies should reassess their inequitable actuarial tables for male and female adolescents.

I did observe that females approached the licensing process with more humility than my son. Cockiness does not go unpunished in government offices. Drew returned in record time from the driving test, having been disqualified within blocks of the station for cutting a corner. His misery was compounded when the clerk told him the test could not be administered twice in one day. The birthday boy responded by kicking over one of the chrome standards that roped us into our ubiquitous lines. "Young man," the clerk shouted after him, "before you control a car, you'd better learn to control that temper."

Later that same day, abetted by his overaccommodating mother and a city street map, Drew located another license station.

This one was bleaker than the first. It was Ellis Island with no chairs or benches for weary parents. Signs instructed us to line up to obtain a form that had been stacked by the door of the previous station. This line took twenty minutes. After filling out the form, we queued up twice more, finally taking a number to await the inspecting officer. We had plenty of time to get chummy with the similarly oppressed. "I hate this shee-it," said the pregnant woman in front of us with the Whoopie Goldberg dreadlocks. "Issa pain in the rear end of my esophagus," she added. We concurred, and by the time we reached the first clerk, Drew and I had learned more than we wanted to know about her pregnancy, her boss, her two nervous breakdowns, and her intention to dump the baby on her mama because she had too much pressure in her life already. We shared a package of barbe-cued chips and sat on the curb of the hot sidewalk while we waited for the test. I watched sympathetically as a teenage girl ahead of us returned with eyes brimming, "The tag, Daddy, the front license tag you put on the car this morning, expired in March. They won't even let me take the test!"

My son had drawn a young blond woman for his driving test this time. Although this day in purgatory had cowed him a little, he winked and gave me the thumbs-up as he slid into the driver's seat beside the inspector. I cringed to hear him call her by her first name and begin his joke about dreaming he'd swallowed a tailpipe and waking up exhausted. When they pulled up twenty minutes later, he kissed her on the cheek and gave me a triumphant high five.

Temporary license in hand, Drew turned on the wrong side of a median, ignored a Stop sign, and overruling my better judgment, drove us home by way of the treacherous LBJ Freeway. He dropped me off at the curb and headed to Burger King for a late lunch without me.

I was exhausted anyway. As I ate my tuna sandwich alone, a certain ambivalence about the day intruded. From that moment on, Drew would be able to go to the pet store he loves, to Eckerd's for poster board and candy, to the video store to check out movies, and God only knew where else without me. He and I have a long history in the car together. In addition to preschool car pools, he had seven years of music lessons twice a week so early in the morning that we could only talk about our dreams or giggle inappropriately at the blue "Uncle Waldo" jokes of drive-time disc jockeys Stevens and Pruitt. His older brother opted early for his bicycle and independence, but this second-born was conveniently the victim of a series of bicycle thefts and got chauffeured through most of middle school. His banter with his backseat buddies kept me from being totally illiterate about sports. I could flippantly toss off astute comments in the barbershop about Cowboys quarterbacks without having to read the sports pages or, worse, having to watch the games. No more. With the windows rolled up, I boogie alone to the golden oldies he always located for me when he had made excessive demands on my chauffeuring services.

Ten years ago, when we lived near the middle school, students frequently discarded homework papers and notes in my yard on their way home from school. I remember retrieving one in which an eighth-grade girl described her mother as being "absolutely clueless." I later read it to my small boys. "Please, guys," I entreated, "just don't let me be clueless."

Through the two older boys' high school days, we played musical cars, since the old one they shared was often in the shop. Several times I was stranded with their car and, with some embarrassment, had to dash to an appointment with "Hot Body" and "Sexy Driver" written in shoe polish on the windshield. I kept lists of grievances every time a son used my car. I have two radio stations that make my erratic days bearable and even pleasurable, the city-owned classical station and our public radio station. A noon errand is less irritating if I happen on the broadcast from the National Press Club. Late-afternoon runs are enhanced by *All Things Considered*. When all else fails, I have French language tapes or a performance by Claudio Arrau of Chopin Nocturnes that I am trying to master. These are four small things that make me happy. I find it inexcusably insensitive that for a quick trip to the drugstore, they reprogram my radio so that it only jumps to head-banging music and that my tapes are tossed out of arm's reach into the backseat.

Boys do leave clues, exasperating ones. I pieced together their unchaperoned lives from the flotsam and jetsam on the floorboard: fast-food wrappers, sales slips, savings-account withdrawal receipts, cryptic directions to faraway football games that I thought were being played at the home stadium, a pair of girl's shoes, an empty can of Skoal Bandits. I drew conclusions and occasionally confronted them.

The response was usually, "Chill out, Mom."

Out? Out of it? I went into this mothering business to go out of it. Their lives were once so open to me that I easily filled two books with our constant togetherness. Now, they control the steering wheel, directional lights, and the accelerator. I am an occasional passenger.

If I've done my job, and their youngest brother quits tattling, my best subject matter just peeled out.

College Tries

◆

The most obvious difference between my high school experience and that of my offspring is not drugs, alcohol, or sex but getting into college. Having gone through this process with two very different sons, I feel like the "Grumpy Old Man," a *Saturday Night Live* character who begins each diatribe against modernity with "Back in my day, we didn't have . . ." My list runs like this: We didn't have SAT's in the seventh grade, tutors for honor roll students, Princeton Review SAT prep courses, private college counselors, "video visits," summers devoted to touring colleges and universities with yearly tuitions higher than my father's yearly earnings, or mothers steaming college envelopes open in April.

As one of my friends recalled, "The only person I talked to about my college options was my Baptist minister. He told me that all of the good Christian young people went to Baylor University in Waco and the other kind went to the University of Texas. I made up my mind on the spot. I had known about as many good Christian young people as I wanted to know in this life, so I headed for Austin." Not much anguish in that decision.

High school college counselors were rare and seldom intruded in the coin toss that dispersed us to various state or private schools around Texas. Sophie Newcomb (Tulane) was about as exotic and far away as the choices got in my graduating class. A friend from Liberty, Texas, tells me that an oddly ambitious counselor in her small high school insisted that she send off for information on the Seven Sisters colleges. "I'd never heard of any of those schools," she said, "but I dutifully wrote letters to all of them. Weeks later I received all of the catalogs except one. My letter addressed to 'Ratliff' had been returned."

Greater sophistication about colleges and universities probably prevailed in elite private schools or in large urban high school in the sixties, but then and now in small towns across Texas not all classmates went to college. Those who did were often satisfied with the local junior college, whose standards excluded no one I knew. Most of us took the Scholastic Aptitude Test once if we took it at all. We thought nothing of attending a slumber party the night before the test. "All I remember about the SAT," says one friend, "is looking up from some exasperating algebra problem to see my best friend, Nancy, doodling her prospective married name over and over in the margins of the math section." Ah, the fifties.

Given our own unpressured experience, I'm amazed at how competitive, how gossipy, and how totally preoccupied with this college business we become by the time our children approach the tenth grade.

My bookshelf suggests my early zeal and eventual declining expectations. Parents of high school sophomores eagerly gobble up books with titles such as *Writing Your Way into the Ivies* or *One Hundred Top Colleges: How to Guarantee Your Acceptance.* By the child's senior year, most of us are just reading books about "letting go" and wondering if we should be talking to the local Navy recruiter.

Even though we know deep in our hearts that motivation and hard work are the only essential qualities for success in college, many of these books and articles exploit our fears that getting in the door involves some gimmickry. We devour chapters on "packaging yourself for admissions" and despair upon reading that some student gained acceptance to Harvard by boldly writing "I Dazzle!" on a glitter-sprinkled page. I dutifully dog-eared and digested everything about colleges I could get my hands on. My sons, on the other hand, never cracked the covers of any of the books except the huge Peterson's directory, which was useful for getting the telephone numbers of admissions offices to request additional applications to replace ones they'd lost or thrown away.

Neighborhood gossip such as "Thad's mom's sister lives there. She says it's a dork school" is readily available at the orthodontist's office or in the supermarket checkout line. Word spreads like wildfire among desperate parents that the way to gain acceptance to a certain university is through its school of education. Teaching aspirations appear from nowhere, only to be supplanted the following week by "environmental concerns" when someone's cousin's nephew whose SAT scores were not great gets "early acceptance" to the School of Natural Resources.

The most important lessons I've learned, however, did not come from books, but from my own experience and that of my friends. I herewith offer our combined wisdom.

Never denigrate any institution of higher learning. At some point every one of us believed our babies would surely someday be pursued by admissions offices from Boston to Palo Alto. In my innocence, I thought it amusing several years ago when my high school freshman responded to taunts in the car pool about taking Honors Spanish by saying haughtily, "You guys have Southwest Conference written all over your faces." Now, even though my husband and I are UT graduates, we do not disparage the state's agricultural and mechanical university with Aggie jokes or even turn down the television volume when the Vocational Training Institute or Truck Drivers of America announces its phone number. Precocious babies often find themselves in the "deferred decision" pool of the Southwest Conference by their senior year.

Listen to the high school counselor's advice with healthy skepticism. Twice I have been advised to simply give my sons their Social Security numbers and turn them loose in the jungle of college applications. The valedictorian, perhaps. Turn the rest of them loose, and college admissions officers will be numbed by essays that begin, "Although I didn't make grate [*sic*] grades in high school . . ." A student who can sift through the mountains of glossy college recruitment literature, keep track of all of the testing and application deadlines, order transcripts, obtain recommendations, set up interviews, ask probing questions of and give insightful answers to college admissions personnel, type, proofread, and make triplicate file copies while maintaining his/her senior class rank is one who may not need to go to college at all.

My determination to let the child handle it was initially undermined when one son returned too early from the PSAT (Preliminary Scholastic Aptitude Test). To his credit, he had the date right, but he had failed to purchase the entrance ticket, which had been sold a month in advance. The older son kept track of the admission ticket for his SAT, but locked it and his keys in his car at the testing site. I rushed out with the extra set of keys and resumed breathing as he bolted for the testing room.

Two months later, when we failed to receive scores, I vehemently challenged the admissions testing person, who suggested that my son had simply failed to take the test. "Look," I said, "there are many things about my sons' lives that I don't know, but I actually witnessed this child going through the doors of the testing room at eight-thirty A.M. on May 5. He took the test!" The admissions testing person responded by mailing me seating charts showing the names of every child who took the test that morning. My son was not present. Under pressure, he confessed that he was three minutes late and the test monitor had refused to admit him. Rather than face my wrath immediately, he just drove around all morning until noon. By failing to confess this promptly, he effectively avoided the next scheduled SAT and had to apply to college on the strength of one test, "a real no-no," according to our ambitious high school counselor. As one incredulous mother said of her son's SAT scores, "No, no, eight thirty can't be your test score. Look again, that must be the time you took the test." I felt better when a friend told me that her son turned two pages instead of one in the middle of the test and "finished" so early that he put his head on the desk and took a nap.

The application process is fraught with minefields, and seventeen-year-old boys are notoriously clumsy. This should be the last reminding, nagging, poking, prodding you'll have to do. It is this process that eases the pain of saying good-bye.

Resist the temptation to write the college application essay. Essays written by mothers are easily identified in admissions offices because they stress what a wonderful home life the child has had.

Pressure to get four or more essays written for fast-encroaching deadlines probably causes more mutual loathing between parent and child than any other aspect of the application process. The parent looks with dismay at the opening sentence, "'One day when I was laying out'? Laying what out?"

the mother explodes. "Four years of high school and you haven't even mastered the use of 'lie, lay, lain,' much less the sense that you don't begin your college essay with a line about sunbathing?" The boundaries of ethics when it comes to the essay are difficult to define. Correcting spelling certainly seems acceptable in an age of computers with built-in spell checkers. I'm even in favor of pointing out incorrect usage in the hopes that one more lesson will do what four years of high school English have failed to do. Suggesting some thoughts when the essay seems devoid of any? Well, I leave it to you. In my neighborhood, speechwriters have been employed.

Start thinking early about the "Honors and Activities" section of the college application. It will require some creativity, especially if your child has demonstrated none in high school. One particularly painful application devotes a whole page with separate sections for Performing Arts and Visual Arts. "Indicate instruments played." (We looked in vain for "stereo" on the list.) Good ol' boys from Texas can leave a lot of white space on the page when asked to indicate the number of hours per week they spend singing, drawing, painting, dancing, or sculpting.

Desperate mothers may find themselves sifting through every aspect of their child's life in search of something that could be called an "outside interest" or "community service." "Jennifer's M.I.P. (minor in possession of alcohol) was a blessing in disguise," one mother told me. "Those twenty hours of documented service that the judge required at the homeless shelter made her look like Mother Teresa on her college application."

Could six weeks of vegetarianism while dieting for the high school drill team indicate an interest in Far Eastern religions? Is driving the housekeeper home a form of inner-city ministry?

Last summer I appreciated my son's friends electing him (in absentia) treasurer of the Young Republicans Club, an organization he'd never joined. Even though we tend to be what in Texas is called "yeller dawg Democrat" in our voting habits, a leadership position on his activities list was tempting. I gave him a character point for declining the honor, but wondered how much leadership potential vice president of the Scrabble Club would convey.

Chant the mantra given to you by the college counselor: "There are no bad colleges, only poor matches." There are, of course, colleges that are difficult to announce with enthusiasm in the parental peer group, especially if you have formerly made sport of graduates of the institution or if the school is so obscure that it requires a great deal of explaining. "We thought Sarah had displayed some talent for hat making when the counselor suggested Stetson University," a father confided.

Most parents are willing to acknowledge early on that their "most precious" may not be Ivy-bound, but through the junior year they harbor some fantasies that the child will somehow slip comfortably into something respectable that they've heard of, such as Vanderbilt, University of Virginia, Tulane, or at least the University of Texas long enough to pledge a fraternity. As SAT scores and class ranks force a sobering reassessment, these parents become a little wild-eyed in their pursuit of schools with more-liberal admission policies or faraway institutions hungry for broader geographic distribution. Engendering some student enthusiasm for these heretofore unheard-of colleges requires some ingenuity. One mother admitted that she considered calling ahead to the admissions office of a small school in Mississippi to ask if they would be willing to position some very attractive young coeds on the steps of the main building to coincide with her son's 3 P.M. interview.

Save money for tuition. Visit colleges/universities after your child has been accepted. The colleges that you detour to visit while you're on vacation are usually the ones *you've* always wanted to see. Although Stanford was not on my son's list of remote possibilities, I couldn't resist wheeling into the palm-lined campus full of fragrant eucalyptus, flowering rosemary hedges, and portentous buildings with this son who at the time seemed interested only in inspecting the weightlifting facilities and cafeteria menus of lesser California colleges. I found the atmosphere on the Stanford campus thoroughly invigorating, even though I had discovered it twenty-five years too late. My son found it thoroughly depressing. The colleges on his list didn't bear up well under the comparison, and I regretted that I had impulsively and selfishly dramatized that fact.

Visiting colleges with your child may underscore the disparity between your perspective on the college experience and that of your seventeen-year-old. Even if the school does not offer separate tours for parent and child, you may feel as if you've visited two different schools. At one school I enjoyed a class on American foreign policy and read bulletin board notices about study abroad while my son observed that half of the kids he met in the dorm were stoned. "You have to look at the posters on their walls and check out their music preferences to get a feel for the student body," he told me. "You also look for buzz fans—means the air-conditioning in the dorm doesn't work."

At the next school, I purposefully headed for the boys' dorm. A bumper sticker in the parking lot set the tone: "Beer, it's not just for breakfast anymore." As the tour guide led us down the hall to inspect a vacant dorm room, I slowed my pace long enough to peer through the open door of an occupied room. The room was a predictable snarl of dirty socks, mildewed towels, and underwear, but I noticed that the desk calendar looked purposefully scheduled. On closer inspection, I saw that the remainder of the year, right through exams, had been marked with daily reminders to "Get laid, get laid, get laid."

Some things a mother should never see.

Go Blue

◆

There is surely no greater pleasure for a parent than watching a child with strong wings fly from the nest. He does not teeter on the edge or look back over his shoulder. He doesn't ask, "Do you think I can do this?" He surveys the horizon confidently and with one swift downstroke of the wings he is aloft and headed for places we've never known—in our case, Ann Arbor, Michigan.

The University of Michigan is usually off the radar screens of college-bound students in Texas. So lonely was the U of Michigan representative at College Night at our local high school that we took pity on her. She had lost patience with the hordes of students and parents who ignored her or just shivered and muttered, "Too cold!" as they passed her table. By the time we picked up one of her pamphlets, she was lashing out, "Haven't you people ever heard of the Eddie Bauer catalog? 'Cold' is a small price to pay for one of the best educational experiences in the country!"

By the time my second son began the college search, I had

changed the rules. To save time and money, I decreed that we would visit institutions of higher learning only *after* they had found our son acceptable. His interest in Michigan had been piqued during a summer session at an Eastern prep school. Although proximity to Eastern colleges was the main reason we'd opted for the expensive Andover summer, Drew's young film teacher, a Michigan alum, persuaded him to skip the college tours by saying, "You belong at a big school like mine. You ought to go to Ann Arbor."

Most of his friends were heading for our own respectable and equally sports-crazed state university. For me, a small-town girl, attending the University of Texas had been a risky and brave venture, a launching out into unknown territory 360 miles to the southwest. My more urbane son thought that the big university in Austin, only three hours down the interstate, might prove to be an academic challenge, but socially, an extension of high school, more years with the same people he'd known for the past eighteen. I admired his willingness to consider casting his lot with new people from places he'd never been—upstate New York, New Jersey, Ohio, Illinois, and, of course, Michigan. Admissions acceptance in hand, we made plans to visit the University of Michigan in early April.

If we had been looking for immediate culture shock, we could hardly have picked a better time. The first weekend in April in Ann Arbor is the annual celebration known as "Hash Bash," when aging hippies (my age) tuck five-dollar bills behind their ears to pay campus fines to local police and proceed to smoke dope and play bongos on the Diag, the central gathering place of U of M. "Is this what it was like in the sixties?" my son asked as we listened to hilarious speeches on the legalization of marijuana. One proponent cited Genesis: "And God created grass and it was good." Another speaker linked weed use to our forefathers, stressing that the Declaration of Independence was written on hemp and that the clothing of colonial America was "homespun," another hemp product. Banners proclaimed: "Hemp for fuel, Hemp for agribusiness, Hemp for fun!" The bongos were drumming and a handful of people were dancing, but on the whole the scene was a parody. Students stood around observing, but mostly drinking Evian and "pop," while the police issued warnings to the elder pot smokers. Without the galvanizing effect of the Vietnam War protest, the trappings of hippie culture just made for a funny spring diversion.

Although Michigan promised to be a totally new environment for Drew, I have never been anywhere with him that he didn't see someone he knew. As we filed into a dorm cafeteria with masses of other high schoolers who had come to tour the school, I was not surprised to hear someone shouting, "Drew Mackintosh!" Ben, a kid from Poughkeepsie, New York, who had shared a house at Andover summer school with Drew the previous summer, joined us for breakfast. Michigan suddenly became an even warmer place.

After the official tour and a visit to an impressive ancient history class, we did some investigating on our own. For such a large school, the campus was surprisingly compact and walkable. We hit the campus bookstores for the obligatory Wolverine hats, T-shirts, and boxers, which clued us in on the regional rivalries. Michigan State was accorded the same derision on T-shirts that Texas A&M gets on Austin's Drag. The "Ivies" received condescending acknowledgment: "Harvard, the Michigan of the East."

At another dorm for lunch, more cultural differences began to surface. Certain cafeteria items were marked with a circled "P." I later learned that these were items that observant Jewish students could eat during Passover. Cafeteria tables were decorated with brief bios of the standard heroes/heroines of multiculturalism—Frederick Douglass, Sojourner Truth, W. E. B. Du Bois, Zora Neale Hurston, and so on. No William B. Travis? Drew and I both were amused that "crossing the border" here meant heading due east to Windsor, Ontario. How seductive could that be?

That evening Drew snared an invitation to a campus party without me. As he tried on his new Michigan cap in our campus hotel room, I shook my head and cautioned, "Looks too eager."

"Actually," he said, "I was going for 'innocent, wide-eyed prospective freshman guy who needs to be taken care of.'" Whatever look he affected must have worked. An attractive blond sophomore took him under her wing the next day for a walk in the university's vast and beautiful arboretum, followed by a sorority volleyball competition played in a soupy mud pit adjacent to the SAE fraternity house.

I chose more politically correct fare, a play called *Sensitive New Age Guys* performed in some campus basement and a noodle bowl at a Vietnamese restaurant counter for lunch. In the original Borders bookstore, a clerk flattered me by asking if I was a new student. When I admitted that I was the mother of a prospective student, he grinned and handed me a copy of British poet Philip Larkin's sardonic poem "This Be the Verse," which begins:

They fuck you up, your mum and dad.
They may not mean to, but they do.

Well, this isn't Kansas, Toto.

If I had any lingering ambivalent feelings about this place, Drew did not. The weather that April was deceptively good; the old buildings, archways, and quadrangles so collegiate;

the school newspaper so fraught with controversy; the fall football schedule and the huge stadium irresistible. A journalist friend who had spent some time at Michigan commented to me later, "The University of Michigan has a sort of intellectual crispness that I think is only possible in climates where April truly is 'the cruelest month.'" On the flight home from Ann Arbor, Drew matter-of-factly dismissed the three fine Southern schools that had accepted him. "I don't even want to visit them. Michigan is it."

On the advice of a handful of Southerners I found who had matriculated at Ann Arbor, Drew and I decided that his academic career there should begin in the fair summer months, allowing him time to establish routes and routines before the wintry blast from the north could blow him off course. I know from experience that after high school graduation, enforcing the house rules becomes futile. Although reluctant to say it, you both know that the old parent/child thing is over and he'd might as well get on with it.

That knowledge, however, did not stop me from making plans to return with him to Ann Arbor for summer school registration. I went off to college alone in 1962, but universities today make it a family affair. Letters from the University of Michigan invited not only the "freshperson" but also his parents to attend orientation, perhaps in hopes of adding more people to the annual fund hit list.

In a last show of authority, I forced him to come home at ten o'clock the night before our departure. "How can I miss seeing the pay-for-view Mike Tyson fight with my friends?" he groused, but he still came home on time. At breakfast on the early-morning flight to Detroit, I was reminded once again that he was beyond my grasp. "Well, I guess it's time to read the poem," he said, retrieving a small blue envelope from his pocket. Looking over his shoulder, I could see that the poem from his senior year sweetheart was dated June 29, 12:15 A.M. "Hey, that's today. Where did that come from? Did she drop it through our mail slot in the wee hours of the morning?" "Nope," he grinned. "I was at her house until about three A.M." What was I going to do about it now? Ground him?

He slept for most of the flight after assimilating his sports scores from the Dallas newspaper. I, on the other hand, used the time to pore over a book called *Inside College,* which I had hoped he would read. Why was I devouring a chapter called "What to Do If Your Roommate Is a Homosexual"?

When we landed in Detroit, I took it as a good omen that our airport shuttle driver was a chatty World War II vet who had been stationed at Lackland Air Force Base in San Antonio. Arriving at the Michigan League, our small on-campus hotel that in times long past had been a separate student union for women, the driver took one look at the heavy army duffle full of Drew's belongings and said, "Big Texas boy can get that one; I carried mine from '42 to '46."

We had just enough time to wash our faces and head to the first convocation of parents and students. With all of the politically correct rhetoric so prevalent in the early nineties, the dean of students, presiding at the Freshperson Orientation, surprised me with a biblical reference from Deuteronomy: "As an eagle stirreth up her nest, fluttereth over her young, spreadeth abroad her wings, taketh them, beareth them on her wings . . ."

She reminded us that the eagle stirs her nest to make it uncomfortable for the young eaglets so they will want to leave. She said that she hoped the parents present had made the home nest prickly enough that these new students would now be ready to "ride on the high places of the earth, to eat the increase of the fields, and to suck honey out of a rock." She explained that it was not the intent of this institution to be a soft landing spot. "The University of Michigan will continue to stir the nest with unsettling ideas and experiences so that they will know that they cannot stay here, either. They must develop strength in these places and move on."

Drew's new nest in Stockwell Hall was potentially prickly. The room was tiny and unair-conditioned. His potluck roommate, Rodney, was a black kid from inner-city Detroit, a basketball player and distance runner. They bonded instantly. Drew did have some concern that his Waylon Jennings country-western tape ("If the South Had Won") might be offensive, and he wondered if Rodney might find the Texas flag he intended to fly from their window and his cowboy boots a little redneck scary. As a gesture of goodwill, Drew claimed the top bunk, where the heat was even worse. When Rodney closed the door to the hall, double-locked it, and put a chair under the doorknob, Drew protested, "Man, this is Ann Arbor, not Detroit." Rodney replied, "Yeah, man, but they some muthas from Detroit down the hall who'll steal your tennies before you know what's happnin'. Keep that door locked." Forgetting it was the nineties, I looked in vain for a housemother.

While Rodney and Drew took advanced placement exams, I had the afternoon to stroll the campus and sample a summer arts festival. Street vendors offered multicultural food—tahini, falafel, and strange herbal teas. No Dr Pepper or nachos here. Could a lone Taco Bell keep a Texan in touch with his roots? Outdoor concerts featured everything from Cole Porter and Gershwin to Debussy and Puccini. I walked past the Undergraduate Library, aptly called UGLI. I stood in front of the Michigan Union and read the bronze marker commemorating President Kennedy's unveiling of the Peace Corps. I read kiosk flyers for every possible interest group and toured the Sigmund Freud Museum. A campus crazy introduced himself as a "black angel" and asked if I had seen the white angels in town. A State Street character called "Shakin' Jake" said I could take his picture. What a splendid place!

Drew and Rodney appeared at my room at the Michigan League just long enough to grab the toiletry purchases I had made for them at a nearby drugstore. Drew reported that he had aced the Spanish placement exam. "Mom, you should have seen the Yankees clear the room when the oral part of the exam began. Sure glad I grew up in a state where a foreign language was available locally." I had half hoped that the comfort of my spacious, air-conditioned room would persuade my boy to spend one more night with me, but supplied with toilet paper, Kleenex, and toothpaste, he bade me good night and said, "Rodney and I need to get *home.*"

I was disappointed when he and Rodney didn't show up for the evening orientation session and dance. This orientation gathering included a rather condescending video instructing those present that calling fellow students "porch monkey, faggot, or chink" could be hurtful. Since my son hadn't appeared, I befriended a fifty-year-old black woman named Donna who was transferring from Wayne County Community College to finish a social work degree. She told me that she was intent on breaking the cycle of teenage pregnancy in her own family. She said, "I am the child of a child and so is my daughter, who also married at nineteen. My granddaughter, well, I want her to be like the young black girls in this Michigan Union ballroom. See how silly and carefree they are! That's the way it should be at eighteen. No babies! No more having to catch up at fifty."

I stayed briefly at the dance, hoping to catch sight of my boy. How could he miss the chance to sign his name to the huge banner that would fly at his graduation four years hence! When he finally appeared, he had no apologies. "You know,

Mom," he said, "this is college. It's not like camp or even like Andover summer school where you have to go to activities even if you don't want to." I was relieved that he didn't think this was camp. A friend's child at the University of Pennsylvania had told her father after her freshman year, "This is just like camp . . . camp with beer!"

The next day we took care of the final details. He met with his adviser, he registered and paid fees. We found a bank, opened his checking account. The banker suggested ominously that I cosign on the account so that if my son died while at Michigan, I could retrieve the money promptly. From the bank, we headed to a bike shop, where I bought him a "maize and blue" bicycle. The clerk must have been a friend of the banker—he recommended registering the bike with the Ann Arbor police so that if my son sustained massive injuries in an accident, his body could be identified. Drew still marvels that he survived four years of college in the nineties without an automobile. Well, I think it's important to have some hardship stories for your grandchildren.

I bought him an organizer notebook with calendar at Ulrich's bookstore, but decided against the three-hole punch. In his new notebook I recorded his phone number, his address, the name of his bank, and most important, the place where he could retrieve his season football tickets. As we strolled through a campus shopping area called Nickels Arcade, a children's bookstore window caught his eye. "Look, Mom, it's *Ant and Bee and the Rainbow.* I always liked those guys. Maybe they ought to go to college with me." I bought the tiny book for him, but I knew I was running out of usefulness. He was treating me. I stocked his small dorm refrigerator with Cokes and snacks, hugged him good-bye, and threatened to write him out of the will if he brought home a girl who said "soda" or "pop" when she meant Coca-Cola.

The airport shuttle arrived on time at my hotel. It made one turn down State Street, which parallels the sprawling Michigan campus. Through the darkly tinted window, I suddenly glimpsed my son on his bright yellow bike now laughing with two new friends I had not met. They barreled across State Street without looking both ways, heading for the Michigan Diagonal and a life I could only imagine. He couldn't see or hear me, but still I tapped on the darkened glass and waved another good-bye, relieved that only the shuttle driver saw the mess I was making of my face.

The Real Mother

◆

Dear Son,

Consider the following:
1. your most recent telephone bill. (Who do we know in the British Virgin Islands?)
2. the overdraft again at the bank. (Just because our bank has changed names again doesn't mean they're not keeping track of these things.) Remember we signed on for room *and board* at the dorm, which does not include daily pizza delivery.
3. the 'C' in "Human Sexuality," purported to be a gut course. (Frankly, I hoped you wouldn't make an 'A,' but the 'C' embarrasses us both.)

Just because your grandmother Ruth is no longer here does not mean that her spirit isn't prodding me to sic the local Army recruiter on you today. Please tell me that you at least use coupons when you call Domino's and that you do not allow the phone company to do the dialing for you.

How about a burst of gumption next semester?

Love (This unconditional stuff is wearing thin.)

    Mom

My mother died in 1996. My sons were almost grown by then, a good thing, because with her went some of the starch and backbone of my motherhood. Knowing that "no non-sense" Ruth Mahaffey was looking over my shoulder strengthened my resolve and made me from time to time tougher on my sons than I might otherwise have been. She, of course, thought I was a complete marshmallow as a disciplinarian.

In my own childhood, she wielded a mean hairbrush. The bristle side was used for wrestling my thick, curly hair into sensible French braids so tight that I looked Asian when I left for school each morning. The flat side of the brush was reserved for attitude adjustment. I was routinely spanked for failure to hang my wet swimsuit on the clothesline, for shaving my legs in the fourth grade, for getting into fracases with my brother, for making my dolls talk dirty, for talking back, for lying, for not staying on my bed for the duration of my polio preventative nap—the list was endless. My brother claims that she is the only mother in history who wrote a thank-you note to the coach at the high school for paddling her son in gym class.

She was certainly not alone in her generation in believing that the slightest indulgence of a child automatically instilled character flaws that would make us burdens to society. She exhibited no ambivalence and brooked no compromises. Like Jehovah, her wrath was swift and sure.

My mother handled all financial matters in our family. It was granting *me* power of attorney three months before her death, not illness, that caused her to throw up when we left the attorney's office. Now that I manage the estate that she accrued through such careful thrift, I dread the Day of Reckoning when she will review my ledgers. I am indulging my ninety-one-year-old father in ways that she would not countenance. This is the woman who told my father in his seventies that he shouldn't buy another pair of shoes because he probably wouldn't live long enough to wear them out and since he had such a small foot, it would be difficult to find anyone else to wear them. What will she have to say about his new stereo system?

I can scarcely remember a single self-indulgence on her part, with the exception of expensive cruises after we were out of the nest. These, of course, were paid for in advance, and I think she harbored some illusion that even these trips were bargains because the cruise lines could not possibly anticipate how much my father would eat at an "all you can eat" affair. This is a woman who hoarded the cotton from aspirin bottles and whose hair salon was the student cosmetology lab at the local junior college.

Not inclined to engage in navel gazing, my mother would probably justify her hard-line mothering as "sensible." Her life until she married had been one of continuing abandonment. Her mother died when she was three, and her father, an alcoholic, left her with immigrant grandparents who subsequently died and left her in the care of an aunt. Her older sister ran away to New York to be a showgirl. Small wonder that her every instinct as a mother was to push us toward self-reliance. If I had difficulty zipping or buttoning a dress and asked for assistance, she would respond, "What would you do if you were on a desert island?"

When I was seven, she gave me two weeks to learn to ride a birthday bicycle that was much too large for me. She intended to buy only *one* bicycle. When I failed to master the beast in the appointed time, she sold it and never bought me another one. I learned to ride the city bus at an early age. "Don't pick her up if you see her at the bus stop," she cautioned her friends. If I called to beg a ride home from school because it was hot and I had many heavy books, my gym clothes, and some science project to carry, she'd sigh and say, "Well, start walking and maybe I'll pick you up." I knew better than to anticipate seeing the family's '58 Olds round the next corner.

A dear friend of mine once told me that her mother never left her presence without saying, "Jean, you are a joy and a pleasure, and I adore you." My mother seems to have sensed early on that the members of our family were collecting enough strokes elsewhere. Her job was to rein it in, to catch me plucking my eyebrows and to trot out the old saw "Beauty is as beauty does." She was critical of parents who bragged on their children. Few things that we did merited compliments from her. She did admire shrewd card playing and regretted that our skill at poker and canasta offered her so little challenge. My older brother claims that one summer afternoon he beat her soundly at a hand of canasta, costing her many points. He says she glared at him in amazement, grabbed the new deck, shuffled it, and said, "Deal." When he won the next hand, she smiled, fixed him a bowl of ice cream, and said, "You just might amount to something after all." Then she said, "Deal," and recouped her losses.

We never felt that we quite met her high standards, and I suppose that fueled some of our striving. Her generous spirit was reserved for those who really needed it, not for her comfortable family. Two years after her death, I accepted a speaking engagement at my parents' church. The minister introduced me by saying that he had wanted me to address this group for many years, but each time he called my mother to get my phone number, she said, "Aw, don't call her. She charges too much and she's not worth it." That was my mom.

As much as I tried to emulate her "straighten up and fly right" toughness as a parent, I have been, in retrospect, the marshmallow. The wisdom of one generation does not always fit the circumstances of the next. She had only one son; I had three.

The small-town world my brother and I inhabited was remarkably benign. Except for the threat of nuclear war, the world we knew seemed a trustworthy and hospitable place. We believed what President Eisenhower told us. Our sports heroes were clean and larger than life. We picked up strangers from the bus stop if they were going our way. Our houses and cars were never locked. Halloween treats were homemade. Nutrition was simply a matter of cleaning your plate. Life, not death, was a deterrent to teenage sex. Marriage was inevitable and forever.

By contrast, my children have grown up with fewer certainties. My first baby was born the week students in a war protest at Kent State were gunned down by National Guardsmen. I nursed the second child while watching the Watergate hearings. Houses and cars are not only always locked, they must have annoying alarm systems. Seeing my youngest sort through sports trading cards gave me a warm sense of fifties déjà vu until I realized that in addition to knowing batting averages and yards gained, he also knew the players' criminal records. William spread his cards on the table and recited incidents of drugs, gambling, concealed weapons, rape, and assault charges. "This one isn't so bad," he said in defense of one of his favorites. "He just cheated on his wife."

My mother's parenting responsibilities did not include monitoring the air her children breathed or the content of their hot dogs. She finished her duties before issues of racism, sexism, pollution, and media violence came on the scene. I prohibited guns; they made them out of Legos. I restricted their television viewing; they watched at the neighbors'. I read aloud to them and got them library cards; they used the books to make racetracks and ramps for battery-powered cars. Adolescence came, and scantily clad *Sports Illustrated* swimsuit beauties appeared on their walls; I countered by purchasing a *Playgirl* magazine and displaying the centerfold "stud muffins" prominently in my kitchen. My sons were duly mortified and probably wanted to have me committed. My mother was proud.

The only other time I can think of that I might have measured up to her standards was the night I busted a high school beer party held in the home of a neighbor who was gone for the weekend. The goofy kids had blacked out the windows with aluminum foil early enough in the afternoon to alert the neighbors on either side that something more than a concern for insulation was up. They lit the house with candles, which by the time I arrived were leaning precariously and depositing stalagmites on antique tables. My sudden appearance sent the kids scurrying like cockroaches, probably to reconvene elsewhere without their keg and without my humiliated son. After helping me put out all of the candles, he was subjected to his mother's smoldering wrath the rest of the evening. When I proudly reported this incident to my mother, I skipped the fact that my reading of the riot act ended with me, not my young felon, in tears. In all of their teenage years, I never achieved outrage without meltdown.

Most of the time I struggled to bridge the gap between my mother's certainty that disapproval, denial, and stingy economies build character and my own growing sense that children living in troubled times also learn from generosity, kindness, and encouragement. It is a balancing act that I still haven't mastered. How could I explain to her that in a moment of madness, I leased a small but picturesque lake house tucked under a cliff in Austin for the undergraduate and his older brother who had returned to graduate school. I had second thoughts when as the fall semester began, the undergraduate's "things-to-do list" left on the kitchen counter of the little house offered these priorities:

1. Buy tiki torches
2. Get dartboard

I scribbled, "Buy books!" across the bottom of the list, and I regularly reminded them that life might not get better than this. My mother would say that I had done them a great disservice by allowing them to experience such a charming abode so early in their young lives. Would their striving be adequate to carry them in this life if we let them in on the not-well-kept secret that they truly are "joys and pleasures" and have had us completely suckered since they were born? More important, would they let us bunk with them at the lake house when we visited Austin?

I still had conversations in my head with these almost grown young men every time I drove to see them in Austin. In these imaginary conversations we discussed important matters of morality and ethics, issues that we never got around to in the earlier years of lost dogs, forced church attendance, football helmets, loose teeth, music lessons, spilled milk, paper routes, sweaty eyes, scraped fenders, charley horses, and letters from camp signed with lumpy hearts.

When we were seated with our Mexican Special Dinners at El Rancho, all of my Interstate 35 profundity was reduced to a hesitant squeak: "Boys, are you . . . are you growing up to be good men?"

"What are you talking about?" William said, upending the Bohemia beer he was finally old enough to order legally.

"Well, I just don't want to become an old lady and suddenly realize that I've raised a son who behaves like Bill Clinton."

"Oh, you don't have to worry, Mom," he said. "I'm not growing up to be the president of the United States."

"Of course not," my mother would have snapped. "A lake house is not a log cabin."

I miss her.

Sons and Fathers

◆

If I gave much thought to the sort of father he'd be, I don't remember it.

I only knew that I had met the guy who made my heart sing. We laughed at the same ironies, met life with similar quotations as English majors, and could think of no moments that we would not willingly share. We were students in love, enthralled with each other's company, and we gave no thought to the family we might someday have.

I didn't know he could quack like Donald Duck or lurch like a camel with two small boys for humps. I never thought to value his very adequate athletic ability or his knowledge of sports. It didn't occur to me to think that his being an only child would make him delight in a disorderly and often chaotic family of five, or that his experience as a surgical orderly one summer in a hospital, in the days before organic chemistry dismissed his medical ambitions, would make him so calm, so curious, and so reassuring in hospital delivery and emergency rooms.

I did value his complete honesty in our relationship, even his refusal to hang around when I declined his first proposal of marriage. He ignored my confused tears, my wishy-washy maybes, turned on his heel, and dropped out of my life completely until I came to my senses. But I had no idea how this high regard for honesty, his unwillingness to cut corners or fudge on anything, would play out in a family. I am the designated social liar in the family. He is George Washington.

Most of all, he was then and always has been a grown-up. Fortunately, he is also a disastrous handyman, a self-punishing investor ("Sell low, buy high"), a contemplative smoker of cigars, an admirer of the rejuvenative qualities of alcohol, an appreciator of women, and an obsessive-compulsive Saturday list maker. I think his sons see him simultaneously as a man of unimpeachable integrity, an efficient problem solver, and a completely predictable nutcase.

He signed on as an equal partner when the babies began arriving in the fifth year of our marriage. He diapered, took rectal temperatures, and walked them when they were sick or resisted sleep almost as much as I did. During the toddler years, he assumed the often arduous evening task of getting three boys bathed and tucked into bed. He knew every inch of their growing bodies and worried about their health and safety much more than I did, an outgrowth of his own hypochondria and his tender heart, which the rest of the family continues to cruelly exploit with terrible practical jokes. When Drew was a teenager, he developed a streaky rash that lingered for two weeks. John, already under the stress of a lawsuit that kept him on the road, dispatched us to the dermatologist, who admitted to being puzzled but not worried. When I reported that the doctor had ordered blood tests, John went predictably ashen.

He set the alarm clock an hour early so he could head to

the office without seeing our streaky teenage boy the next morning. "I can't bear to look at him or talk to him until we have a report on that blood work." When the report showed nothing disturbing, my co-conspiratorial son suggested, "Let's whack Dad out completely. Call him and tell him that I'm being admitted to the hospital for a few days of observation."

We weren't that naughty; I know better than to tempt the fates, and I remember how kind he was to me when the tables were turned. Once when I was off on a magazine assignment in Arizona, this same son inhaled a pen cap while solving a crossword puzzle. (Well, I once bruised my chin by continually poking it with a pencil eraser while trying to come up with the right word on the computer screen. Words are dangerous.) John handled the emergency hospital run and kept me calmed down by long distance, downplaying what I now know was a very scary bronchoscopy procedure.

He is the parent who issues the boring litany of caution each time the boys depart. "Buckle your seat belt, drive safely, use your head, do the necessary, wear sunblock . . ." I'm glad that when they were younger, he missed their rolling into the gutter after faking a bounce off the hood of my car when I picked them up after school in the afternoon. The poor crossing guard never got used to this ritual. The fair-skinned youngest still delights in calling his dad to report bogus sunburns after a day on the lake and to falsely register how many minutes he shaved off his record drive time on the return to Austin.

The Mackintoshes are actually, with few exceptions, risk-averse folks. Drew once rafted the rising Turtle Creek with a younger neighborhood friend in a child's inflated wading pool during a violent thunderstorm, narrowly missing being swept into the storm drains. He was so pumped with adrenaline when he returned from the adventure that all I could say was, "Why didn't you take me with you?" Most of the time we take our risks by failing to floss or letting the dog run without her leash.

The boys will probably never appreciate as I do the time their father devoted to their early years. He often had lunch at his desk so he could accomplish more at the office and still be home at five-thirty to help me. I could never have launched a writing career at age twenty-nine had he not taken charge on the weekends, allowing me to spend hours in my tiny garage office working without interruption. Most of his male contemporaries spent their Saturdays at the office, on hunting leases, or on golf courses.

As boys our sons seemed bent on resisting everything he tried to give them. Men don't seem to agonize over their children's initial lukewarm responses to their leisure passions. They just give it to them with both barrels whether they like it or not.

As his grandfather had done for him, John eagerly took all three boys fishing as soon as they were old enough to hold a cane pole. They returned from most of these outings swearing they'd never go again. "It wasn't the fishing we hated; it was Dad," the inveterate anglers now recall. One began fishing in earnest on his own in high school, finding and finagling his way onto fishy private waters all over North Dallas. The youngest waited until he got to college in Austin, but now rarely goes anywhere without his fishing gear in the trunk. Their father holds no grudges about their earlier behavior. He's just pleased that somebody in the family is at last always up for a trip to "Fishing World."

On more than one spring break, he took all three boys skiing while I stayed home to luxuriate in the peace and quiet or to finish a writing project. What do they remember of these sojourns? "Canned creamed corn!" they chorus. It was a staple of their father's kitchen repertoire that invariably appeared without their vote on these outings. It was especially memorable the year they all got sick in a motel in Utah. "It's awful, Mom," Jack told me when I called to check on them. "We're all hurling corn and Dad doesn't care. He's making Drew keep his head in a wastebasket cause he didn't make it to the bathroom." Dad also gets credit for getting them in a public hot tub in their underwear. "You don't need bathing suits. Nobody else will be in the hot tub at this time of night," he promised, as the four of them dashed toward the tub in their tidy whites. A party of women, of course, arrived just as they were about to exit. "We looked like Sun Maid raisins, but we outlasted them," the humiliated eldest reported.

Also memorable was the trip to the beach with Dad when they packed so haphazardly that William turned up at the first rest stop shoeless. Rather than purchase new shoes that would be unused at the beach, the thrifty Scot decided that since he had two pairs, they could just pass their shoes down. The older two, who were currently communicating their coolness with status tennis shoes, nixed that idea. I wish I had a movie of the compliant youngest, skating through Luby's cafeteria in his father's size ten loafers.

He did not coach their sports teams. Trial lawyers who are at the beck and call of clients can rarely control their schedules precisely enough to take on such duties. He did, however, play a lot of catch, throw passes, and shoot hoops with them in the driveway, giving no quarter. Because they frequently came in from these competitive sessions bunged up or in a snit over some critical suggestion their father had offered about how to improve, I would have happily dispensed with such outings to promote peace and tranquillity. How many times would I hear, "I hate Dad. We got the wrong kind of daddy!" As a pre–Title IX woman, I had no interest or appreciation for the role sports play in adolescent development, especially male development. I figured that every Texas male got an overdose of sports by osmosis; sports participation needed no encouragement and certainly no pressure from the home front. We attended their games, but we didn't hire pros to coach them or dispatch them to highly competitive sports camps in the summer. I wanted them to be broadly educated, well-read young men with something to talk about beyond Monday-night football. They now tell me that I was wrong, wrong, wrong about that. We do not live in Boston. I now realize that male friendship in Texas, if it develops at all, probably begins with team sports. Deep in the heart of almost every Texas male is some small feeling of inferiority if he did not endure high school "two-a-days" in the August heat. On Fridays in Texas, the guys who sit on the stage at the pep rally still rule. Mea culpa, not Dad's.

Together, they saw Rangers baseball games, Mavericks basketball games, and plenty of football, pro and college. They knew their dad's unexpurgated opinion of every player. Before they could drive, he even volunteered to take them to rock concerts, but, of course, made them leave when the foul and abusive language was more than he could stomach.

If they complained that their father was short-tempered and blunt with them and, worse, with their friends, I always reminded them that they were comparing him with "Miss Congeniality" herself. I brought to this union an overdeveloped ability to make everybody comfortable. If I had not been drawn to an opposite, they might have drowned in the excessive affability.

I also remind these ingrates that they are the recipients of the fruit of his labor as a lawyer. He is trained to assume nothing, to seek the truth, and to be suspicious of everyone's motives, even theirs. My own father, a pussycat by comparison, once commented, "Don't those boys of yours get tired of being cross-examined?" Small talk or "passing the time of day" is not my husband's forte. He wants a full report from his sons. I encourage them to edit for entertainment value; their father begins his debriefings with, "You left Sunday night at eight and . . . ?" He wants unembellished testimony replete with timetables and names of witnesses.

Perhaps because he does not squander his affections on everyone he meets, those of us who are the recipients of his devotion often get more than a full measure. He goes to the video store, rents *The Barefoot Contessa* and tells his sons, "You probably didn't know that your mother had a movie career before you were born. Her stage name was Ava Gardner." He is my personal shopper. He willingly hits the malls to slap the racks in search of a stunning dress for me, always spending more than I would have spent had I gone alone. If my sons ever wonder what love looks like, I will point to the day we cleaned the attic and discovered that a rat had chewed the stuffing out of the old Raggedy Andy dolls and teddy bears, well-worn sleeping companions of an earlier day that I was saving for future grandchildren. The devastation of the ripped faces, of dangling button eyes, and especially Freddy Bear's torn-away nose, the juxtaposition of childhood innocence and nasty violence, made me irrationally hysterical. The boys seized on this opportunity to flee the attic chore, leaving their dad, who had carted a load to the alley, to deal with the madwoman in the attic. "Dad, you better get up there. Rats ate the butt out of the Andys, and Mom is having a nervous breakdown." Six months later, the incident long forgotten, I opened a big box under the Christmas tree to find the lovingly restored Andys and bears ready for a new generation of droolers after their convalescence at a faraway suburban doll hospital. What a guy!

Although we have tried to steer our sons clear of that air of entitlement that inevitably crops up in children for whom life has been a bit too comfortable, I still feel that they take much of what their dad has given them for granted. Once a week family Mexican food fixes often ended with John on the drive home saying sarcastically, "Thanks, Dad, we really enjoyed the dinner." I don't blame him. He's been incredibly patient waiting for their gratitude. They have never entered his presence without getting hugged, even when they were at their prickliest. With his legal skills he has walked and talked them through a few fender benders, and he has given them better representation than they deserved in traffic court. If academic credit were given for the hours spent in defensive driving classes, my sons would all have Ph.D.'s by now.

Now that they are venturing into the larger world, John's sage advice on job interviewing is just barely tolerated. Like a broken record he cautions them: "When you see Mr. S_____ tomorrow, remember to be very respectful. He's the head of the company, and you should feel privileged if he gives you ten minutes of his time." "Yeah, Dad, like I was planning to slouch into his office and say, 'Hey, *vato,* how's it hanging, man?'" One son, who exhausted our every employment lead and finally landed his job by pounding the pavement in New York, once called to inform us, "You know absolutely nothing about getting a job!"

They feign similar respect for his advice on women. After years of monosyllabic non-conversation with boys, John and I both are so hungry for a daughter-in-law that we are generally kept on a short leash when young women stop by. John has always pointed out the young women he admires. He is especially smitten by girls with "smart eyes" who put themselves through school with waitressing jobs. "You can guess that she's not spoiled, and if times were hard, she'd be willing to take a job at El Chico to make ends meet." Some of the girls he picks out for them, I am pleased to note, bear a strik-

editions of a daily paper meant that my dad was not much inclined to help with Boy Scout badges in his leisure time. After my mother died in 1996, my brother admitted that he had trouble writing letters just to Dad. He had always written for Mother. Funny, I had always written for Daddy.

My father was not a handsome man, but he never knew it. I couldn't view either of my parents objectively enough to assess their physical attractiveness. Was my mother pretty? I don't know. Both of their faces were too intimately imprinted on my brain as My Parents, as though they belonged to a separate category of beings who looked, well, exactly as they should look. In the earliest photographs I have of my father, excluding those Edwardian baby portraits in a long white dress holding on to a metal chair, he is about three years old and wearing his "Milwaukee suit," a short-pants outfit with a broad-brimmed hat. In this photo, he is adorable "Bud Tot," as his much older siblings called him, ready to sing "I'm Forever Blowing Bubbles" to soften up the stern Victorian attorney whom he called Papa. He was the indulged baby in a family of four children. In her early forties at his birth, his mother, an active suffragette, left him in the care of a black servant so frequently that his dinnertime recitations of the day's activities often had a decidedly black slant. His recounting of a trip to the circus included so much exclaiming over the derring-do of "that white man on the high trapeze" that his father drolly asked his mother, "Susie, does our son know he's white?"

My father was vain. I never saw him pass a mirror or shop window without cutting his eyes to admire his reflection. He was about five feet seven, baldheaded from the time I knew him, a little overweight and stoop-shouldered from hours spent writing and rewriting news copy on an old L. C. Smith manual typewriter. He had protruding teeth so bizarre and crooked and discolored that even if orthodontic treatment

ing resemblance to the woman he married, but he is certainly not immune to the charms of the six-foot-tall blondes who have occasionally graced our dinner table. While my sons may dread the gentle cross-examination their dad invariably gives their dates, they must know that those who bear up well under his scrutiny are generally "keepers." I have watched young women who initially seemed to be all hair-tossing dazzle and breathless baby talk suddenly square their shoulders under his gaze and converse with considerable intelligence and honesty.

Despite the boys' resistance to his advice, I know that they unconsciously absorb much more of his view of the world than mine. Gender matters. An equal partnership in marriage does not necessarily mean that sons inherit equal measures of parental influence. Their father is a great dancer, but he does not play the piano, sing, or—most galling to me—read novels by women. Neither do they. Physical characteristics are more evenly distributed. All three have his height, one has John's nose with my chin and another has my eyes, his chin. Whose recessive genes brought blue eyes and the two southpaws? All three lament that they have my embarrassingly narrow wrists. Strangers seem to recognize in them resemblances to us and to each other that I can never quite see.

The interior attributes are harder to sort out. Has his dour Scot strain weighed more heavily on the firstborn or is this son simply the product of birth order, the child of our inexperienced expectations? At certain points in their growing up, I observed talent, but worried that they had no drive. Or I detected drive, but saw no recognizable talent. Sometimes, I just thought they were so adorable that the world would require of them neither talent nor drive. The balance of their father's perspective, his long-term view, his refusal to agonize over problems we couldn't or shouldn't solve for them, his ability to identify predictable maleness where I saw pathology, and his reassurance that the best we could do would be good enough makes me sympathetic to men or women who must rear their children alone. Educator Urie Bronfenbrenner has compared family life to a Ping-Pong volley, the bantering, the giving, the forgiving. He says it needs to be a constant tapping out of the rhythm of life, sending the steady message pulsing through children that somebody is nuts about you. Single parenthood must be like constantly serving with no one to return the ball when it misses the mark or rolls off the table.

Their dad's love and respect for me, his lifelong affection for Mexico, his longing for trout streams, his no-nonsense Episcopal grace before meals, his insistence that they pay attention to the bright orange dragonfly dipping into the backyard fountain, the goldfinch on the bird feeder, and the owls at dusk, his nonnegotiable rules on gun safety, and even his quirky little alley vegetable garden will undoubtedly resonate in these young men's lives much deeper and longer than all of the music lessons, art museums, concerts, and plays I foisted on them.

If he gets the extended pleasure of their adult company now in fishing boats and on golf courses, he's earned it. In fact, he's probably still paying for it.

Last Dance

◆

On a bookshelf just above the television set is my [photo]tograph of my father and me. My father is seven[ty] photo, and I am thirty-seven. I am wearing a wh[ite] and my father is in his tuxedo. We are dancing. [A magazine] had assigned photographer Matthew Savins to ill[ustrate an essay] I'd written called "The Way to a Woman's Heart[." Despite my] father's anxiety about being photographed in th[e studio, when] the photographer put on a recording of 1930s l[ove songs] somewhere between "Someone to Watch over [Me" and "The] Way You Look Tonight," he captured the lifelo[ng mutual ad]miration society of a father and a daughter.

My father would be the first to admit that he [was not the] father for a boy. He couldn't throw a ball and [had no interest] in the outdoors unless it was groomed for p[lay. When my] brother was born in 1938, before my father [. . .] members the year Santa didn't come because D[ad, the newly] minted editor in chief of the *Texarkana Gazette*[, lost the Christ]mas money in a craps game with the printers.

ing resemblance to the woman he married, but he is certainly not immune to the charms of the six-foot-tall blondes who have occasionally graced our dinner table. While my sons may dread the gentle cross-examination their dad invariably gives their dates, they must know that those who bear up well under his scrutiny are generally "keepers." I have watched young women who initially seemed to be all hair-tossing dazzle and breathless baby talk suddenly square their shoulders under his gaze and converse with considerable intelligence and honesty.

Despite the boys' resistance to his advice, I know that they unconsciously absorb much more of his view of the world than mine. Gender matters. An equal partnership in marriage does not necessarily mean that sons inherit equal measures of parental influence. Their father is a great dancer, but he does not play the piano, sing, or—most galling to me—read novels by women. Neither do they. Physical characteristics are more evenly distributed. All three have his height, one has John's nose with my chin and another has my eyes, his chin. Whose recessive genes brought blue eyes and the two southpaws? All three lament that they have my embarrassingly narrow wrists. Strangers seem to recognize in them resemblances to us and to each other that I can never quite see.

The interior attributes are harder to sort out. Has his dour Scot strain weighed more heavily on the firstborn or is this son simply the product of birth order, the child of our inexperienced expectations? At certain points in their growing up, I observed talent, but worried that they had no drive. Or I detected drive, but saw no recognizable talent. Sometimes, I just thought they were so adorable that the world would require of them neither talent nor drive. The balance of their father's perspective, his long-term view, his refusal to agonize over problems we couldn't or shouldn't solve for them, his ability to identify predictable maleness where I saw pathology, and his reassurance that the best we could do would be good enough makes me sympathetic to men or women who must rear their children alone. Educator Urie Bronfenbrenner has compared family life to a Ping-Pong volley, the bantering, the giving, the forgiving. He says it needs to be a constant tapping out of the rhythm of life, sending the steady message pulsing through children that somebody is nuts about you. Single parenthood must be like constantly serving with no one to return the ball when it misses the mark or rolls off the table.

Their dad's love and respect for me, his lifelong affection for Mexico, his longing for trout streams, his no-nonsense Episcopal grace before meals, his insistence that they pay attention to the bright orange dragonfly dipping into the backyard fountain, the goldfinch on the bird feeder, and the owls at dusk, his nonnegotiable rules on gun safety, and even his quirky little alley vegetable garden will undoubtedly resonate in these young men's lives much deeper and longer than all of the music lessons, art museums, concerts, and plays I foisted on them.

If he gets the extended pleasure of their adult company now in fishing boats and on golf courses, he's earned it. In fact, he's probably still paying for it.

Last Dance

◆

On a bookshelf just above the television set is my favorite photograph of my father and me. My father is seventy-five in the photo, and I am thirty-seven. I am wearing a white lace dress, and my father is in his tuxedo. We are dancing. *Texas Monthly* had assigned photographer Matthew Savins to illustrate a piece I'd written called "The Way to a Woman's Heart." Sensing my father's anxiety about being photographed in this stark studio, the photographer put on a recording of 1930s love songs, and somewhere between "Someone to Watch over Me" and "The Way You Look Tonight," he captured the lifelong mutual admiration society of a father and a daughter.

My father would be the first to admit that he was not a good father for a boy. He couldn't throw a ball and had no interest in the outdoors unless it was groomed for playing golf. My brother was born in 1938, before my father grew up. He remembers the year Santa didn't come because Daddy, the newly minted editor in chief of the *Texarkana Gazette*, lost the Christmas money in a craps game with the printers. Getting out two editions of a daily paper meant that my dad was not much inclined to help with Boy Scout badges in his leisure time. After my mother died in 1996, my brother admitted that he had trouble writing letters just to Dad. He had always written for Mother. Funny, I had always written for Daddy.

My father was not a handsome man, but he never knew it. I couldn't view either of my parents objectively enough to assess their physical attractiveness. Was my mother pretty? I don't know. Both of their faces were too intimately imprinted on my brain as My Parents, as though they belonged to a separate category of beings who looked, well, exactly as they should look. In the earliest photographs I have of my father, excluding those Edwardian baby portraits in a long white dress holding on to a metal chair, he is about three years old and wearing his "Milwaukee suit," a short-pants outfit with a broad-brimmed hat. In this photo, he is adorable "Bud Tot," as his much older siblings called him, ready to sing "I'm Forever Blowing Bubbles" to soften up the stern Victorian attorney whom he called Papa. He was the indulged baby in a family of four children. In her early forties at his birth, his mother, an active suffragette, left him in the care of a black servant so frequently that his dinnertime recitations of the day's activities often had a decidedly black slant. His recounting of a trip to the circus included so much exclaiming over the derring-do of "that white man on the high trapeze" that his father drolly asked his mother, "Susie, does our son know he's white?"

My father was vain. I never saw him pass a mirror or shop window without cutting his eyes to admire his reflection. He was about five feet seven, baldheaded from the time I knew him, a little overweight and stoop-shouldered from hours spent writing and rewriting news copy on an old L. C. Smith manual typewriter. He had protruding teeth so bizarre and crooked and discolored that even if orthodontic treatment had been available in his youth, I do not think anything short of extraction could have improved their appearance. Did I mention that he stuttered? He had very small, soft hands and wore a size seven shoe. An odd bone disease, Paget's disease, bent his left shin as he aged in such a way that my mother speculated that archaeologists would someday dig him up and think they'd found an Indian artifact.

In spite of his teeth, his height, his stuttering, the young man who became my father was a Jelly-bean. My dictionary doesn't define this long-gone slang term, but young J. Q. "Buffalo" Mahaffey did. It had nothing to do with his elliptical balding head or the sweetness of his personality or his penchant for repeating a hilarious and humiliating story about the bell captain's white gloves and the case of homemade blackberry jam in the trunk of his car at the Waldorf-Astoria to anyone who mentioned the city of New York. "Jelly-beans" were the male equivalents of the Roaring Twenties flappers, best known for their sharp dressing and flirty flattery and their ability to dance the Charleston. Born in 1907, my dad came of age relatively privileged in the twenties with the Jazz Age and Prohibition. I look at old photos of my hometown and picture him jerking soda at Gallagher's or loitering with his Sixth Street gang in front of Jimmy's Confectionery, all thinking they were the "cat's meow." He remembered the first Model T's, the substituting of electric lights for the gas fixtures in his house on Olive Street, and World War I recruits drilling in front of his house near the post office on State Line Avenue. He was a regular at the local movie theater. His earnest attempts to emulate the menacing squint and swagger of Tom Mix, his favorite silent-movie cowboy, often caused his father to suggest that perhaps the boy needed a purgative. He conjured up for me such a clear picture of his boyhood in Texarkana that I sometimes forget that the trolley tracks he mischievously soaped were long gone when I was born in 1944.

His father sent him away to Columbia Military Academy for high school. He returned the first Christmas resplendent (he thought) in his uniform with cape and saber and headed straight for a popular young lady's house. Her new boyfriend answered the door and yelled over his shoulder, "Nancy, there is someone here to see you. I think it's the postman."

He went away to Furman in a yellow convertible and blew a great deal of his father's money intended for books on booking Ted Weems's orchestra into the local hotel in Greenville, South Carolina. F. Scott Fitzgerald defined "Jelly-bean" as "one who spends his life conjugating the verb to idle . . . I am idling, I have idled, I will idle." In a small-town Southern way, my dad walked right out of a Fitzgerald story in his raccoon coat. His college yearbook pictures him as "biggest sheik" and "best dressed" and describes his leaving a trail of broken hearts all the way to Converse College in Spartanburg. So vivid were his tales of leaving a dollar on a rural porch and returning later to retrieve a Mason jar of "moonshine" that I sometimes think I lived the whole century with him. He knew our hometown when it sparkled with new wealth from the timber industry, and he could re-create for me the glamour of summer dances on the roof of the Grim Hotel, where tall electric fans blowing over tubs of ice cooled the perspiring dancers.

The Great Depression and marriage to my smart, no-nonsense mother cut short Jelly-bean's idling days, but he retained his dapper style, his ability to flirt, and his soft Carolina accent. He never doubted that he had married a woman of superior intelligence. Friends often compared my parents to George Burns and Gracie Allen, except that they reversed the roles. Daddy was Gracie.

My first encounter with my father was recorded in his newspaper column, in speeches, and in our countless introductions of each other at public events through the years. The story goes that on seeing my unfocused eyes just after I was born, my father cornered the family doctor and said, "Give it to me straight, Reavis, she's blind, isn't she? Dr. Picket replied, "J.Q., the child is less than an hour old. What do you expect her to do? Write an editorial?"

That was my father's job for most of his life, writing editorials. His journalism career, first as a reporter, then as editor of the *Gazette* and its afternoon counterpart, the *Daily News,* spanned four decades, from the crash of the stock market in 1929 through the Lyndon Johnson presidency. He chased bank robbers Bonnie and Clyde all over Red River County, interviewed Will Rogers, worked 'round the clock to get out World War II reports and contended with the FBI, Texas Rangers, and national and international press when they were all drawn to our town in the forties by a series of still unsolved murders. Reporters dubbed the unapprehended criminal "The Phantom Killer," and my father gave interviews on these events well into his nineties. By marrying a fellow reporter at the *Gazette* and by keeping her on the staff sporadically even after I was born, my father saw to it that I grew up amid the heat, the grime, the smoke, and the excitement that was a 1950s newspaper office. Almost everyone and everything of interest in town came through the doors of the newsroom. I met every president from Truman through Nixon. I also saw clubwomen, civic leaders, preachers, circus folks, and regular townspeople, proud or grieving, all in search of some notice for themselves or their children. Old Associated Press and United Press International wire service machines rang bells to announce incoming stories. The whole place fairly vibrated with a sense of urgency. Typewriters clacked, ashtrays overflowed, coffee grew cold and rancid, and telephones never quit ringing. The aging society editor, Annie Mae, frequently became so engrossed while gathering the latest gossip that she inadvertently set her frizzy hair on fire with a burning cigarette in the hand holding the telephone receiver to her ear. "Somebody put Annie Mae out!" a reporter would yell, and another would beat the singed locks with a telephone directory. More heat from hot lead poured into the window-less, unair-conditioned newsroom each time proofreaders handed copy through the sliding glass window to the type-setters in the clattering composing room.

Overseen by a penurious, eccentric publisher, the news-room was rife with absurdities. Dank toilets in a dark hallway were supplied with a roll of newsprint in lieu of real toilet tissue. Memos from the publisher about wastefulness were often followed up by his ferreting out discarded pencil stubs in trash baskets, sharpening them with a pocketknife, and returning them to the offender's desk. My father maintained that his requests for small raises were always met with, "Why, John Quincy, if I hadn't hired you, do you know what you'd be doing now? You'd be a ribbon clerk at Ben F. Smith's." Years later, when I lauded my father's hiring of women to cover police beats and city council meetings at a time when women were usually confined to reporting teas and fashion shows, he burst my feminist bubble by explaining, "Oh, honey, I had to hire them. They'd work for less."

My father loved the news business, and, as a family, we al-ways felt sorry for the "outsiders" who would never know the funny, cynical, irreverent camaraderie of newsrooms or the tri-umph of getting the story and being on the inside of almost everything that happened in our town. No pretentiousness was attached to writing in my family. It was a taken-for-granted motor skill that my brother and I enhanced by writing letters that were sometimes returned to us proofread and corrected.

In lieu of gifts, my father wrote a love letter to my mother each Christmas, an especially touching one the year he gambled away Santa Claus. He could write and edit a hard news story, but he remained an old softy with a sentimental streak that touched his readers and kept the father/daughter dance going his whole life. When I was ten, he wrote a column that began, "If a man has ambition to grow in character as the years rush by, I can't think of anything he needs more than a daughter." And when he was eighty-nine, we sat in the kitchen of my parents' house, both exhausted by the frustrations and sadness of my mother's final illness. He looked up from our cold supper and said, "You know why I'd like to live forever?"

"Sure, Daddy—so you could wear out that Brooks Brothers sport coat I gave you for Christmas and watch the Masters Golf Tournament every spring."

"No, so I could keep on loving you."

Small wonder that my father was never without some romance in his life. He liked women, and right to the very end, he expected them to like him. Secure in a marriage that lasted until she died at eighty-six, my mother tolerated, even encouraged, his flirting, as he tolerated hers. He was always falling in love with a choir member at the church, absolutely certain that the soprano soloist sang just for him.

In his nineties, without my mother to deflate his ego, he worried that his friendship with a bright young *Gazette* reporter who occasionally took him to lunch or a movie might be mistaken for something more. "You kids don't need to worry. Your inheritance is secure. I'm not going to get married again, even if she is pretty sweet on me," he said.

When his poor old bent back and breathing problems made it difficult for him to shuffle outside his apartment, romance came by mail. It started with a condolence note from Cousin Kay, known to me only as Uncle Presley's daughter.

Several weeks later, as I routinely sorted through Daddy's accumulated mail, cards from his Sunday school class, long, hilarious letters from his old newspaper buddy George, and AARP magazines, he reached for the stack. "Don't read these. They're sort of mushy," he said, stashing several letters with decidedly feminine handwriting on the envelopes in his desk drawer.

He had not seen Kay Corley since 1922, when he was fifteen and she a year older. Her letters brought back one of his sweetest memories, a dreamy Christmas afternoon in Clarksville, Texas, at Aunt Mattie Marable's. He remembered her beautiful strawberry blond curls, and she remembered how handsome he was in his Columbia Military Academy uniform. They danced all afternoon in the parlor to the Victrola, and at the end of the day, noting his moony expression, his mother jerked him up and said, "You do not fall in love with your first cousin!"

With no one left to object, the "dance" resumed seventy-six years later. Her husband, Bill, had been gone for many years, and my mother had died in 1996, sending my father into a deep depression. I give Kay's lively letters as well as the prayers of Baptists and Carmelite nuns as much credit for his recovery as I do the miracles of pharmacology that his young psychiatrist prescribed.

Kay's correspondence from Cuero, Texas, where she had moved to be with her daughter, invariably began with the salutation "Dearest sweet man," or "Honey." They were full of picturesque recollections of relatives they shared, picnics in the piney woods, and sometimes they ended with resolve. "Let's kick and wiggle as long as we can even if our derrieres aren't quite what they used to be."

I knew from another cousin that Kay's health was at least as bad as my dad's, but reading her sweet and funny letters (he eventually had me read them aloud to him) buoyed us both. During the four years of their "romance," my father's physical health steadily declined. At one point, I asked him if he'd like to see Kay. I thought some time away from his retirement apartment might do him good. I was prepared to make the trip from Texarkana to Cuero leisurely, with plenty of bathroom stops and lots of picnics along the way. His answer surprised me. "Oh, no, honey, I don't want to see her. She probably looks just like these old women who live here. I like the way I see her right now. She's sixteen, so lovely and graceful, a wonderful dancer."

As he grew weaker, her letters piled up on his desk. He reproached himself for not answering them, an unthinkable breach of etiquette to a South Carolina–educated gentleman. He apparently wrote her one last letter the week before he died. When I cleaned off his desk after his death, June 29, 2000, I found her reply.

My dearest, sweet J.Q.,

I have just received your letter marked finis, final, exit, deadend, point of no return. Of course, I understand it, honey. You closed the door, never to be opened again, my love. That is all right with me, but you forget that I'm a very diminutive person and I can easily crawl in a key hole and there I am—aha!

Do you think for one minute that I can't realize the discomfort you have, the efforts to breathe that you are making? Oh, but I do and it breaks my heart. Certainly I'll not intrude on the private battle you are having just to say I love you, sweetheart. If I have one outstanding trait, it is compassion. Thank God for that, but it means also that I hurt for you.

So now I'll go quietly and tiptoe out of your life

all the while thinking beautiful thoughts of the boy
I loved once long, long ago.

Your devoted,
Kay

You'll understand why I sometimes have to pull off the road when I flip through the easy-listening station on my car radio and hear, "Heaven . . . I'm in heaven. And my heart beats so that I can hardly speak. . . . And I seem to find the happiness I seek . . . when we're out together dancing cheek to cheek."

Dog at the Manger

◆

We're into heavy petting at my house. The consummate frat guy who announced in 1963 on learning the name of his blind date, "Aw, girls named Prudence are always pushovers" was right. My most recent indiscretion, against all of the better judgment that my name implies and the wisdom of my fifty-six years, has produced a fourth son, Cisco. He came to us about the time tech stocks became doggie. His nobler name is FranCISCO, for the saint who blessed the animals and made them a part of the Christmas creche. Cisco is an eight-week-old chocolate Labrador retriever with very blue eyes that follow me like those eyes of Jesus in the Sunday school room picture. His still-small head rests on my foot while I type this.

I can give you a dozen reasons why I did NOT need or want a dog at this time in my life. My last child had just graduated from college, and if the economy continued to expand he would be off our payroll in a matter of weeks. We were freer to travel than we'd ever been. I had writing assignments and a lovely third-floor office in which to do them. I have never been lonely in my own house, which is filled with books I intend to read and a piano that beckons like an old lover. Having similarly unencumbered friends over for dinner no longer required a frenzy of cleanup, since two adults create relatively less clutter than a family of five once did. The chain-link fence in our backyard had been replaced by attractive stonework and holly hedges. I had even decided to quit dressing like a soccer mom.

So why am I working here at my small kitchen desk in a sweatshirt with my shoelaces untied, surrounded by a half-shredded oatmeal box, a couple of rag bones, and a chewed Oriental rug held together by pet stain remover, all on a hardwood floor that is gradually being bleached by dog urine and shellacked by puppy slobber? Will, the recent graduate, peers into the metal crate in the kitchen where Cisco slumbers peacefully in the evening to Schumann's "Cradle Song" and asks, "Mom, is that a pillow he's sleeping on?"

"Of course. Did you think he was a dog?"

Dogs, or "dorgs," as the late John Cheever dubbed his household rulers, have always come into our lives for totally irrational reasons. I can barely remember "Cinder" or "Evan Llewellyn Evans," much less their provenance. Some cocker spaniels named Buttons and Bows, later in my youth, were gifts from a dog-crazed relative who had rescued them from Mexico. My college roommate and I briefly kept Feo, a mutt with a serious underbite that we'd found in the alley behind our sorority house. While John attended law school and I taught junior high English, we lived with his grandfather in Austin. In addition to his little dachshund, Siggi, who could catch malted milk balls in midair, Papa frequently agreed to train other people's bird dogs. A particularly difficult speckled pointer named Ginger became expert at fetching my underwear from the clothesline. After parasailing around the block with my bras, she invariably abandoned them on a shy widower's side porch. A full-grown female Shetland sheepdog adopted my young sons after school one day and we kept her until we found the ad in the paper from her owner. Our reward for returning her, was, of course, one of her pups, an American Kennel Club–registered sheltie whom we named Rosie. Rosie happily herded our boys, but also urinated on the floor each time my husband greeted her and spread the mess with her fluffy tail. She succumbed to epileptic seizures after only six years.

We had been dogless for more than ten years. My husband, who hunts perhaps twice a year, had begun to wax rhapsodic about his friends' sweet dogs who worked the fields so diligently flushing quail. I could tell that he could do with more tail wagging at the end of the day than I'd mustered lately. It had been a bad year. My father's failing health had kept me exhausted, running back and forth to Texarkana every other week, and the life we shared in Dallas had dwindled to a sort of coping survival in which we did the necessary but little else.

The advent of Christmas, as it usually does, found me wandering with vague lists at the mall in the midst of decisive women who seemed to be wrapping up their last stocking stuffer before I'd even begun. I was easily distracted by the animal shelter's display. Rusty, a full-grown border collie mix, nuzzled me gently and looked as if she'd fit comfortably into my sedentary routine. I made a few obligatory purchases and went home to discuss possible adoption of this sweet abandoned dog with my sons, who had been goading me to "make Dad really happy for Christmas."

The sons were predictably horrified. "Mom, you're not adopting some mixed-breed mutt for Dad. What did they do at the mall? Post a sign above Rusty's cage that said, PLEASE TAKE ME HOME. THEY'RE GOING TO KILL ME ON CHRISTMAS EVE?"

"No, but you know that's what will happen."

"Mom, Dad wants a real dog, a dog that can go hunting with him. Get him a man's dog, a Lab."

I vacillated as the days till Christmas dwindled. Shirts and socks were piling up as ho-hum presents under the tree. When my youngest son saw me wrapping cedar suit hangers for John to discourage moths in his closet, he began circling the classified ads and making not-so-discreet calls. "Where exactly is Kaufman, Texas, Mom?"

I checked out books from the library on pup ownership. In the years since we had owned a dog, experts had published an entire shelf of exhaustive works on the care and feeding of young canines. All of my previous dogs had survived the rather haphazard care we'd offered, but these books spoke of tooth brushing and creative play four times a day as de rigueur. Anyone for "plastic soda bottle soccer"? I left the books lying around for my pressuring sons to peruse. Their response was the same one I fell for so many years ago: "Aw, Mom, it won't be so hard. Besides, Drew and I live right here in town now. We'll do everything. He can run with us, and we'll take him to the park for Frisbee. You won't have to do anything."

Note that the dog was always discussed as "he." I had insisted that the sheltie pup of their youth be female to even up the gender discrepancies in this predominantly male household. This time I agreed to fall in with the majority. Perhaps our female sheltie's epilepsy had been an understandable response to the excessive testosterone at our house that kept her constantly trying to unscramble rivalrous boy bodies from the nightly wrestling matches that preceded bedtime. After my thirty years with male offspring, I concluded that a male dog would have difficulty surprising me. Love the one who feeds you, mark your territory, grab the last cookie, and torment your siblings. Be a little goofy, honest, and adorable, and chicks, even your own mother, will fall for you again and again. I know the drill.

From talking to friends with Labrador retrievers, Will and I had all of the buzzwords down pat. We knew to examine the puppy's ears and to ask about hip dysplasia. Puppy sellers were all over the pre-Christmas classified pages, but none anywhere near our zip code. We set up evening appointments to view two litters on the Wednesday before Christmas. At the last minute, Will and I decided that we couldn't keep this search a secret. I wanted my husband to share the responsibility if we selected the wrong dog.

The first litter greeted us on the porch in Arlington. Six or seven little chocolate bears tumbling over each other while their handsome mother, still recovering from their cesarean birth, licked and nosed them to look sharp and get themselves adopted. They were irresistible. Viewing a second litter in Grand Prairie suddenly seemed absurd. We handled every pup, or maybe we picked up the same one over and over again. I couldn't tell them apart at all. The owner swept one little fur ball out of the bunch and pegged him as the bully, the one who was constantly mixing it up with his brothers, nipping their ears and tails until they joined in the fracas. My son and husband immediately liked him best.

Twilight was fading, so before we made our final choice, the amiable owner allowed us into her house to look at the pups in better light. She apologized profusely about the odor and filth. I assured her that anyone with three children, a litter of ten puppies, and a full-time job need not apologize. "They're already paper-trained," she said proudly. "How would she know?" my son murmured under his breath. As we surveyed the depressingly devastated house, the word "litter" took on new meaning. Our eyes watered from the strong ammonia aroma that rose from the cluttered floor. I moved a sticky high chair tray on the table to sign the AKC papers attesting to the noble bloodlines of the pup, son of "Shelby Jo" and "Skeeter."

I admired her Christmas tree, the only thing in the house that appeared unmolested, as we gathered our coats, our new pup, and a baggie with enough puppy chow to get us through the night. "Well, I hope you sell them all and have a very prosperous Christmas with the profits," I said as we started for the door.

"Oh, there won't be no profit," the owner said. "We still owe the vet $775 for Shelby Jo's cesarean. Two of them pups' bags just popped inside of her, and we had to rush her to the emergency clinic to get the rest of 'em out."

Great, I thought. *We have just written a check for a pup who was probably oxygen deprived.* Instantly I envisioned our vet saying, "Mrs. Mackintosh, can we step into my office?" And once I was seated, he'd say, "I'm so glad this puppy has a mature home to go to. He's going to require the sort of love and care that a lot of people just don't have the patience to give. You've probably noticed that he's blind. He'll lose the use of his hind legs before he's eight weeks old, and of course housebreaking him is out of the question, but with your constant care, he'll be a difficult, but very devoted companion for your golden years."

The night was cold and clear. Our plans to grab some Mexican food between litters gave way to a burger drive-through, a harbinger of sacrifices to come. As we reached our suburban neighborhood with its extravagant Christmas lighting and manicured lawns, Will said, "Well, Pup, you're in the Bubble now. You'll have to learn to eat with a fork."

At home, I cleared my desk of the careful notes on assessing litters and stacked the puppy manuals for return to the library. Cool, cautious deliberations fly out the window when

puppies are present. How could I have forgotten that this til death-do-us-part commitment is invariably sealed under the intoxicating influence of sweet puppy breath, the cheek kiss of a tiny pink tongue, and the unfocused gaze of trusting blue eyes? With absurd bravado, this handful of thick, soft fragrant fur on stubby legs with paws three sizes too big and satin ears whimpered his first command at the back door, squared his little shoulders, raised his head to take the scent of the cool, clear December night and tumbled down the back steps straight into our hearts.

Quiet!!!

◆

Many years ago I occasionally took walks with an older woman in my neighborhood. She told me that when she was a young mother and her noisy household seemed overwhelming, she sometimes announced that she needed to go to the bank. At the bank, she would purposefully head for the safety-deposit-box basement, take her unopened box to a private cubicle, and just sit and luxuriate in the silence. "It was so restorative," she said. "Now my whole house is like that safety-deposit-box cubicle, and someday yours will be, too."

My last kid moved out this weekend. The milk in the fridge is already blinky. Since his college graduation, he'd occupied our garage apartment, as did his older brothers after graduation while looking for a job. In those few months, we became so accustomed to his good-natured presence that we were a little surprised when one evening on our way to eat Mexican food, he abruptly said, "Could you just stop the car here? I think I'll just jog back to the house and eat something there."

The prospect of another meal with the parents was suddenly more than he could face. Time to go.

Now that the silence of the safety-deposit-box room has descended, there is some rearranging to do. It's time to close out the permanent record card, blots and all, and bring back the girl/woman I once was. My sons' triumphs and camouflaged missteps belong on their résumés, not mine. The persistent dilemma of motherhood, when to push and when to let the chips fall where they may, is not resolved, but it *is* over.

If it were possible to shed the role of mother altogether, this is the time to do it. Mom needs to recede. She learns not to call a son's office or at least to pose as a client when the receptionist asks, "Who may I say is calling?" She does not drop in to straighten diplomas on his wall, even if she has a meeting in his building. As much as she'd like to trade her mother persona for that of wise and interesting older friend who happens to know his entire history and who always has his best interests at heart, she is always his mother. The world is not kind to young men who hang out with Mom.

They, of course, are slow to learn that I am no longer available to get their cars to the body shop, to make their dental appointments, to locate the missing tuxedo jacket, or to iron a shirt for the next job interview. Because . . . mea culpa, I am.

Dads seem to slip effortlessly out of their patriarchal roles and onto the golf course with grown sons. The Mackintosh foursome can compare miserable golf swings or talk about the stock market. Dad even slips a little "flash cash" in their pockets or surrenders his best Rangers tickets if they're dating someone he likes. But who wants to see Edith Wharton's *House of Mirth* with Mom?

I shouldn't complain. They were most intimately mine for nearly two decades. They put the Play-doh in my typewriter keys that initially frustrated, then fueled a career. By no prior design, I became the Boswell for lives that in no way resembled Samuel Johnson's.

Our eldest was the most complicated. Is there any first-born who has entirely forgiven the intrusion of subsequent siblings? He was our happy, performing, outgoing toddler until his brother Drew showed up. I can still see him standing beside my rocking chair while I nursed the new baby. With tears streaming down his formerly jubilant little face, Jack said, "Momma, he don't want it . . . he don't want it."

Our relationship has had its ups and downs, probably because of unrealistic expectations on both sides. He bore the brunt of new-parent zeal and returned the favor with occasional critiques of our own inadequate performances. This is the orderly firstborn child, who at age nine, probably after retrieving his gym clothes from the dryer, announced that he'd like to trade his haphazard mother for the reliable routines of an orphanage. I couldn't learn to be a mother fast enough for him. I was always turning his underwear pink in the laundry, showing up at his elementary school on my rusty Huffy bicycle with my hair in dog ears, or doing old cheer-leading routines with my friend Anne beside his soccer field. He wanted structure; I wanted him to loosen up. He wanted an operating manual; I wanted poetry.

He and I took a trip to Washington, D.C., when he was twelve. The differences in our memories are telling. I recall a totally unleashed moment when, without umbrellas, we got caught in a torrential downpour at the Washington Monument. Hair plastered and dress soaked, I peeled off my shoes and ran hand in hand with him, fording puddles and laughing all the way back to the sedate Hay-Adams Hotel. In the lobby, he immediately regained his composure and shuffled this soggy, giggling, disheveled mother into a swift empty elevator that whisked her out of sight.

His memories of the trip? The Smithsonian flight museum? The White House? No, he claims to remember nothing of the Washington part of it. He fondly recalls, however, the side trip to Wilmington, Delaware, where we stayed with my college friends. Their only son, two years older than Jack, owned a "badass" electric guitar and gave him a stack of lightly worn Ralph Lauren Polo shirts, a much-coveted brand that this frugal mother had steadfastly refused to buy. In your face, Mom.

When he was eighteen, not a great year to travel with your mother, we spent four days together in and around San Francisco, touring colleges. I knew we were off to a bad start when Jack and I butted heads in the airport over his wanting to play video games while we waited for our flight. From the moment we stepped off the plane, he resisted looking at anything I deemed interesting. Eighteen-year-olds are much too cool to be tourists.

Under duress, he joined me on the cable car to Fisherman's Wharf. While I admired the subtly painted bay windows and the Chinese man in Union Square performing his tai chi regimen in a business suit, my son averted his eyes from the always breathtaking view of the Golden Gate Bridge and counted Porsches and BMW's parked on the streets. My East Texas penchant for engaging complete strangers in conversation weighs heavily on this taciturn child, so on this trip I contented myself with eavesdropping. A young boy on our cable car pitched a fit when his mother refused to let him hang off the side and drag his foot in the street. The genial cable car conductor ruffled the boy's hair and said, "Aw, Thomason, they plan this whole trip around yo' good behavior and you done blown it awready." I renewed my determination not to let my own son's churlish behavior ruin this trip. How could we not share a chuckle when our drive to Haight-Ashbury included a stop at an Asian market called

"Phuket's"? Steiner Aquarium allowed him to gaze wordlessly at sharks and giant groupers like Dustin Hoffman's graduate, and in San Francisco, of course, there is always lunch. I observed no foot-dragging when it was time to queue up at Caffe Sport in North Beach for the shrimp in aioli sauce or Yuet Lee's for seaweed soup. Both sites served up ample distractions, so that our sparse conversation was hardly noticeable.

By the fourth day of the trip, we agreed to go our separate ways. I had tickets to a play, and he wanted to go to the legendary original Gold's Gym. Three hours later I returned to an empty hotel room. I spoke with the concierge about the location of the gym and learned that it was in a most unsavory neighborhood. "Your kid went there alone?" I sweated another hour in the hotel room envisioning my son's encounter with Hell's Angels, his battered body in a gutter.

When he strolled into the room unharmed an hour later, he was downright loquacious and willing to do what we call in our household "tell it like a girl." I got the full picture of the gym. Beefy, sweating men with dreadlocks, tattooed guys on deadly steroids, a kindly gym manager who lent him a weight belt, the variety of motorcycles defiantly parked out front in a No Parking zone. "This one guy had incredible back muscles. I asked him how long he'd worked for that. Six years!" Algebra II be damned! "So how did you get home?"

"Well, I had to walk a long way before I found a cab. The cab guy was really weird. Actually, kinda cool. He said he's a poet who went to San Francisco State. He knew that guy we talked to in Admissions yesterday. First he chewed me out for walking around in such a sleazy neighborhood, then he quizzed me on what we'd seen and done. When I recited the colleges I'd visited, he said, 'Okay, so you've wasted your high school years. What now? Look, I don't give a shit what you think of me. You're never gonna see me again, but if you're counting on college to catch you up, you're in trouble. What are you reading? College is important, but in four years it can't give you the world you need to see. You've got to start this afternoon and read, read, read.'" A San Francisco cab driver with a reading list. Angels unaware.

What I interpreted in this son's high school days as stubborn wrongheadedness, I sheepishly acknowledge now was actually his unwillingness to be me, to see the world the way I saw it, to love the things that I loved. His independence, his determination, his drive, even the gym workouts, have served him well. What's not to admire about a guy who has had a paying job since he was fourteen? He left me in the dust by getting a graduate degree and a job in New York. Truce is declared. If I concede that my upper arms could use a personal trainer, he might take me to the Vermeer show at the Met and let me sleep on his sofa.

The late cartoonist Al Capp, creator of Li'l Abner, used to draw a character named Joe Bfstplk with a permanent rain cloud over his head. If I were able to draw our son Drew, it would be with a perpetual sunny day surrounding him. Even now when he travels, previously miserable weather seems to clear just as he steps off the plane. His years at the University of Michigan dictated almost undefeated football and basketball teams. He moved to New York and the Yankees won the pennant. The Texas Longhorns made a comeback when he entered graduate school in Austin. It was ever so. As a teenager, he caught fish at night in the dead of winter. I can still see his cocky fifteen-year-old face, his toothbrush handle wagging in his mouth like W. C. Fields's cigar as he greeted the assembled breakfast crowd, "What can I say . . . what can I say? January 26, five-and-a-half-pound bass." His envious little brother countered with the only ammunition his nine years could muster: "You know, Drew, you're so ugly with that freckle by your mouth. It makes people sick to watch you eat."

"This freckle, Willie, my man, is a sex device."

This son's great gift, however, is not his Cindy Crawford freckle. It is his uncalculated generosity. Even in pursuit of a selfish endeavor, his cup invariably runneth over so there is something for everybody. He is our unwitting goodwill ambassador. He high-fived the school janitor and schmoozed store clerks at the mall, who in turn saved perfume and cologne samples that he gave us for Christmas. He sat in the front seat with cab drivers on our vacations in Mexico to practice his Spanish and saved us all from Ugly American status with his easy banter.

His fishing gear was always in the trunk of his car, and he could sniff out fishy water in the most unlikely suburban setting. On one occasion when access to a small private lagoon seemed impossible, he simply knocked on a door. A housekeeper answered. Looking like a latter-day Huck Finn, he said, "I really need to fish that water behind your house, but I can't see any way to get on it except through your house." "Well, I have to ask Mrs. Mason about that," the woman replied. She motioned him to the back of the house, where he met Mrs. Mason, an elderly, bedridden lady. Once an avid fisherwoman herself, she immediately granted his request and had the housekeeper help her into her wheelchair so she could see him from the window. Each time he caught a fish, he ran it up to her window and then released it for another day. The odd friendship and the fishing rights continued for the remainder of his high school days.

He accompanied me once on a speaking engagement to Vicksburg, Mississippi. Known primarily as an encyclopedia of sports statistics, this fifteen-year-old surprised me as we strolled the battlefields by providing color commentary on

Union and Confederate generals in the Civil War, known locally as "the Wah of Nawthen Aggression" or the "Late Great Unpleasantness." He knew details of Grant's forty-seven-day siege of Vicksburg and the significance of having had an ancestor who had survived in the caves on the bluff. At the museum, he exhausted his bargaining skills on a bemused docent in hopes of getting one Confederate uniform button out of the display case for a souvenir. He disappeared later in the afternoon while I was napping. My first thought was that he'd returned to the museum to work on the docent again. He offered no apology when I finally spotted him blocks away from our bed-and-breakfast, shooting hoops with four black kids at a peach basket goal nailed to a telephone pole. He just grinned and said, "Cedric says we can stay with him the next time we come to Vicksburg."

The world continues to be hospitable to Drew. He makes it look so easy.

Will, Willie, Willyum, Wildo, Wildeaux (during our French phase), Mimo (during our Mexican phase), the much-put-upon and much-blessed baby of the family, assumed "only child" status at fifteen, the year his second brother left for the University of Michigan. To his brothers, he is Jacob's Joseph or Benjamin, the child of our older and far more generous hearts. To Jack and Drew's claims that "the baby got it all," I have to plead guilty. As an elementary school kid, he was the child with whom I would not have let my eldest associate. He was the worldly wise third child who had access to high school humor and X-rated movies rented by older brothers who often were his baby-sitters. He was supervised by worn-out parents who no longer believed that the survival of Western civilization hinged on their attendance at parent meetings called "Circles of Concern." This child *did* have a curfew; we just couldn't stay awake for it.

In an earlier book, I recorded the gradual withering of my resolve by noting that this was the child who threw a tantrum at the grocery checkout stand and actually got the chewing gum. I once took pride that my epitaph would someday read, SHE NEVER BOUGHT SUGARED CEREAL, but on a Christmas break from college, the older boys spotted the Frosted Mini-Wheats in Willie's bowl, not to mention an entire case of soft drinks, which he seemed to pop open at will. They were outraged. "What is this? First you get cable TV. Now this, Mom? He's ruined. We went off to college overwhelmed by the freedom to eat Sugar Pops and drink a Coca-Cola whenever we wanted it"—I had rationed one soft drink a week—"He'll be whining that the beer in the keg isn't imported." Automobiles seemed to be another measure of this sibling's undeserved favored status. Jack and Drew were carpooled in an old maroon Chevrolet Caprice with a peeling vinyl top, a car so unattractive and hopelessly out of place in a neighborhood of shiny new imports that the police once knocked on our door to ask if it was an abandoned vehicle. Baby Will came into our lives the year we bought our first new car. When he turned sixteen, the brothers were again outraged that he was driving a car he actually chose, an old but very "in" Ford Bronco. Where was the hand-me-down, character-building, canary-yellow Chevy Malibu that had seen our eldest through college? He likes to remind me that the 1971 Malibu had slick tires, no air-conditioning, back windows that wouldn't roll down, and an interior so torn up that foam pieces had to be brushed out of his hair each time he emerged from the driver's seat.

The older siblings also believe that I perpetrated "smile inequities." Jack worked to pay for his own orthodontic work and wore braces in college because I had refused to believe that he actually had a "crossed bite." Drew really didn't need braces, but still thinks we owe him at least three thousand dollars for keeping the mouth he was born with. Will, of course, went to the orthodontist the year that all of his classmates were "metal mouths" and emerged two years later with a million-dollar smile, to which the older boys attributed his subsequent unwarranted social success. (He actually had a girlfriend in high school.)

"I must have been on crack to agree to this," fifteen-year-old William remarked the summer he and I settled into a grand old colonial house on Calle Cuadrante just off the main square in San Miguel de Allende, Mexico. Church bells from the multi-spired pink-granite Parroquia church seemed to ring randomly, roosters crowed, street food vendors selling fresh corn on the cob kept up a steady litany of *"Elotes, elotes . . . ,"* and motorcycles roared in the dusty streets, but once inside the massive wooden doors to our rented place, total peace reigned. A refreshing courtyard fountain splashed water on the surrounding potted geraniums and a cold pitcher of *limonada* appeared. Tiny barn swallows had nested in the thorny crown of Jesus on the massive wooden crucifix just inside the door, and cascades of bronze-colored bougainvillea spilled over the terra-cotta-colored wall near the lighted niche housing the ubiquitous Virgen de Guadalupe. It is still the *casa* of my daydreams.

We were there to study Spanish at the Academia Hispano Americana. I had had no formal Spanish instruction; he had had a couple of years. His plan for the summer, I soon realized, was to see what might stick with zero effort. I, on the other hand, had lugged the five-pound verb book in my purse so I could master *"estar"* and *"ser"* before the plane landed at the airport in Leon.

I can think of few things more abhorrent to a fifteen-year-old boy than sitting in a Spanish class with his zealous middle-aged mother, who has resorted to being the sort of smarty-pants sixth-grade girl that she probably once was. I saw him wince each time I raised my hand to clarify a pronunciation or to ask, "Aren't you going to take up the homework?" Will quickly learned to feign *turista* and escape to the house to watch ad nauseam a Kirk Douglas/Martin Sheen war movie, the only offering on the single English-speaking TV channel. By the second week, I arranged for us to be in separate classes.

In six weeks, I advanced to intermediate status with some fifth grader from Midland, Texas, and a bunch of Oregon schoolteachers who were as earnest as I was. Will happily remained with beautiful Gabriela in a beginning class that goofed off by wandering about town drinking hot chocolate, buying flowers in the market, and eating ice cream. Mexico never judges and always accommodates.

I still walk those streets strewn with jacaranda blossoms in my dreams. Does my son remember that summer of *"elotes,"* the stone-faced blind beggar, the dog with the underbite, the solemn religious processions with Jesus wearing a purple satin dress, or the guitars in the *jardín* with any affection? He pauses, then says, "Yeah, that house was cool. I used to smoke cigarettes on the roof after you went to bed." I am certain that he improved his Spanish, even though subsequent report cards at his high school belied the fact. While cleaning his room after he'd left for college, I found a box full of girlie magazines in Spanish dated "julio 1992." Such treasures must have required some *español* bargaining in the *mercado*. I had to get out my dictionary to read the articles.

I am happy to stop paying college tuition, but I bid farewell to my sons' college days with some sadness. How does fall begin without fresh spirals? I loved the vicarious pleasures of perusing course offerings, savoring reading lists, occasionally going to classes they found mildly interesting. While their dad was the higher-achieving English major in college, I am the one who still reads the stuff and loves it. In our library, which now clutters three floors of the house, I can always lay hands on Donne, Yeats, Byron, or Keats. Emily Dickinson sometimes rides in my glove compartment. Edith Hamilton's *Mythology* is as dog-eared as my first cookbooks, and thanks to my Baptist upbringing, I can spot a biblical reference in the most obscure poem or work of art. Even now I am a member of an anachronistic group that reads Shakespeare and writes papers on the plays and sonnets just for fun. I was ever the reference librarian for my sons' last-ditch efforts, the one who probably aided and abetted their procrastination. Their college experience introduced me to contemporary authors I might never have read, Chinea Achebe, Italo Calvino, and Leslie Marmon Silko. If I despaired over my sons' occasional lackluster academic performance—all ignored my suggestion that they tether themselves to an earnest Asian student for four years—I never doubted that they were at least absorbing the astonishing absurdities and the variety of mankind that a large university invariably offers.

Jack wrote letters from college so funny that I've saved them for use in his own novel someday. When I heard about a midwinter "naked run" tradition at the University of Michigan on a public radio news program, I called my own Wolverine, Drew, to ask if he had witnessed the event.

"Witnessed it? I ran in it."

"Naked?" I gasped.

"Of course not. I wore my cowboy boots."

The youngest brought me news of rest-room graffiti at the University of Texas. The graffiti usually reflected the discipline taught in the building. Hilarious syllogisms appeared wherever philosophy was taught. The art building, of course, had the best graphics. The newer buildings, with rest rooms designed to prohibit any wall art at all, required ingenuity.

The only available writing space in the Sanchez building facilities was the grout between small tiles. The space dictated carefully printed inscriptions such as:

"Grout House"
"Three strikes and you're grout."
"Here is my handle and here is my grout."
"Groutso Marx"

In subsequent buildings, where slicky faux marble replaced the tilework, a plaintive protest in indelible laundry marker appeared: "Oh, I miss grout!"

Our conversation is necessarily trivial these days. We exchange brief summaries of work lives and their apartment hunting, weddings among their friends. That's exactly as it should be. Motherhood in an all-male family really never had as much "heart to heart" talk as I expected. It was mostly small accretions of seemingly trivial words and deeds. I can count on one hand the things that I'm certain they consciously learned at my knee:

(a) a nonsense lullaby my daddy sang to me (Kimo, nero, delsy, karo?)
(b) the Twenty-third Psalm (the nightmare chaser)
(c) the proper use of "lie, lay, lain" (you cannot be "laying down" unless you have had congress with a duck)
(d) a unique finger-snapping trick that gained them some notoriety in middle school.

Should they need a refresher course on any of the above, they've got my number. I'm not waiting by the phone. In the tranquillity of a safety-deposit-box cubicle, Boswell will surely find new subjects.

Something Fishy

♦

No one expected me to like it. This fly-fishing trip had been on the calendar for almost a year. With only the last of my three sons still in college, I could no longer claim motherly responsibilities or financial concerns as an exemption. I kept my misgivings about the vacation to myself. My husband is confident that when the pearly gates swing open, we will see Montana in the summertime. When lawyerly stress threatens his sleep, he mentally places himself in the cold, clear stream and lets the rhythm of the water and his casting send him Letheward.

His euphoria over my willingness at last to accompany him on a fishing trip was too apparent for me to confess that I was banking on excessive snow runoff from the Rockies to cancel the whole thing. Late June, after all, is a bit early for optimum river conditions on the Smith. With the rains in Montana still falling a few weeks before our departure, I could afford to be a cheerful good sport, borrowing waders, boots, and rain gear from women friends who already had embraced fly-fishing with enthusiasm that I never expected to feel. I even allowed my husband to give me some rudimentary casting lessons in the front yard, in full view of the neighbors. This trip would never happen.

Standing on the banks of the Smith River on the twenty-second of June, I met my companions for the week. The Montana River Outfitters included six young men who would see that our party of eight caught fish, were kept warm and dry, and were well fed for the whole week of camping along the river. These were capable and uncomplaining guys who probably shared my unspeakable dread at their having to ferry yet another novice woman through this idyllic wilderness. Our fishing party comprised two couples and four men who had left their wives behind. Five of the men knew each other from previous fishing expeditions in Canada and Russia. We knew only the other couple, good friends who had been transplanted to Atlanta. Anne, my only female companion for the week (unless you counted Brooke, the amiable black Lab who traveled with one of the river guides), is an accomplished fly fisherwoman. For that matter, I can't think of anything she does at which she is not accomplished. She grows orchids and very smart children. She speaks French so impeccably that once on an international flight, a Parisian seat companion, after much conversation, asked if she also spoke English. I wasn't surprised to learn on this trip that she also ties her own flies and steadfastly refuses to fish with anything other than dry flies made with no synthetic material. A boon companion, yes and no. She was as intense about the fishing as Alan, another member of our party, who fastidiously cleaned his line between casts all week.

The Lewis and Clark National Forest ranger who seemed like a cast member from the movie *Fargo* lectured us briefly and earnestly on the river conditions. Was I the only one in our party disturbed by the fact that the river was running at a velocity of 1,800 cfs (cubic feet per second) when it should be running at 300 cfs? We could still go back to Great Falls and tour the house of Western artist Charles Russell, which we had missed while the men were buying more last-minute gear.

My husband was too excited to listen to the ranger. The sun was out, and the rest of the party was easily reassured by predictions from our outfitter, who wasn't exactly eager to refund our money, that the velocity of the river would drop 300 cfs per day. We separated our gear into what we'd need for the rest of the afternoon and what could go on ahead with the guides who would set up camp at our first stop. My afternoon gear included my son's felt fishing hat secured to my head with a pair of shoelaces, a sketch pad and assorted colored pencils, and a book called *Little Rivers: Tales of a Woman Angler.* I figured if I couldn't do this, I could at least read about it and join in the conversation.

Despite the sunshine, the water that first afternoon was swift and high and very cold. Jim, our first guide, rowed against the current to slow our boat enough for my husband to cast into the "slick" near the weeds on the bank. The rapid flow seemed far more suited for sport kayaking than artful fishing. Our four boats were spaced far enough apart on the river that we immediately had the illusion of being absolutely alone.

Having recently read Stephen Ambrose's *Undaunted Courage,* I settled in to see this river valley with its thousand-foot canyon walls and soaring osprey with the same goose-bumpy freshness with which Lewis and Clark had seen them nearly two hundred years earlier from their dugout canoes. Captain Lewis, who strolled the riverbank after dining on elk killed nearby, remarks on the river's beauty in his journal entry of July 15, 1805, and records that his party named the river in honor of Secretary of the Navy Robert Smith.

The headwaters of the Smith rise in the Castle and Little Belt Mountains, ranges formed by raised fault blocks exposing basement rock nearly three billion years old. Spruce and Ponderosa pine trees seventy feet tall shoot skyward from the unlikely ground, sedimentary rock shelves hundreds of feet above our heads. I blunted all shades of my green and brown pencils trying to capture enticing Indian caves and clear springs pouring out of the sides of the cliffs over moss-covered rocks. Meadows full of primrose and wild iris and a lovely but destructive golden weed that the guide called yellow spurge exhausted my pink, purple, and yellow pencils. Nobody warned me how many cerulean blues the Big Sky would require.

While the guides set out a late picnic lunch on the bank, Anne and I scouted out the ladies' room behind a distant bush. Hearing the men comparing notes on the relative merits of colored strike indicators, I felt vaguely superior. Not confined to keeping eyes at water level, I was bound to have an experience on this trip that would be undeniably richer than theirs.

We settled into our first night's camp early enough to take a brief hike up to a lovely meadow. Our awkward, heavy-booted presence in this unsullied stretch of grass interspersed with delicate wildflowers made me think that somewhere in the brush, Bambi's mother was whispering, "We can't go into the meadow today, Bambi. Man is in the forest." Time spent in this pristine part of Montana could make a tree-hugging environmentalist out of the worst beer-can-tossing Texan.

Back at camp, we broke out the wine and hors d'oeuvres while the young men who had rowed against the current all afternoon began dinner preparation. Cocktail conversation this first night was quintessential male talk of previous exotic fishing trips, possible future exotic fishing trips, and the ever more perfect gear that they had brought on this trip. There was no letup during our sumptuous dinner of halibut steaks and fresh asparagus. It was "show and tell" night, and I had nothing but clearly inadequate borrowed girl stuff that wasn't worth showing. Bait fishing at Girl Scout Camp High Point in Mena, Arkansas, in the fifties just didn't come up. The men eyed me with some suspicion when I announced that we'd better have the camp dance early in the week before we all smelled too bad. My brain numbed at the thought of having to listen to tales of fishing the Mirimichi for six nights running. I was glad that I had brought my books and a small clip-on reading light.

John and I retreated early to our cozy two-person tent. As one whose idea of roughing it was formerly La Quinta, I was surprised at my immediate affection for our spiffy tent. The dome-shaped shelter was floored and double-skinned, with zippered screened windows and a skylight. The height was adequate for men well over six feet. The efficiency and simplicity of my multi-zippered camp duffel bag was equally satisfying. I had packed well, which meant I had enough clean underwear and socks, so that I never minded wearing the same outer clothes every day. My jacket stuffed in a pillowcase was a perfect pillow. My jeans were draped across the foot of my cot, and my new hiking boots, of which I grew inordinately fond, stood by the bed as slippers should I need to hike to the distant latrine during the night.

A few words about the latrines in this Smith River portion of the Lewis and Clark National Forest, because women want to know these things: At each camp we found a sturdy, well-secured freestanding single latrine with a real toilet seat, not enclosed but always thoughtfully obscured by natural vegetation or by rustic man-made screens that always afforded the occupant a pleasant view. One latrine required a real cardiovascular hike up the mountain, but the rest were just a pleasant stroll away from the campsite. The first night, the guides recalled that the last time they had stopped in this particular boat camp, previous visitors had dumped their left-over pancakes down the latrine instead of packing them out. "The bears just tore that latrine clean off its platform going for those pancakes," Bryan the guide told us. Hmmm . . . pretty hungry bears.

Hearing of the bears' visit to the latrine, my husband promised to accompany me on any necessary night trips to it. He snored so peacefully that first night, however, that I couldn't bear to wake him. I groggily slipped into my jeans and boots, grabbed the lantern, and hiked off by myself. Returning to the tent, I quietly unzipped the front and then fumbled with the flashlight lantern, trying to turn it off before the glare awakened John. Fortunately I was pushing the wrong button as I barged into the tent, for just as I was about to flop on my cot, the light fell on an unfamiliar body. I had stumbled into Walt and Alan's tent, and only my ineptitude with the flashlight had prevented my crawling in with Walt. Neither of the men awakened, but it was certainly a conversational alternative to talking about hatching caddis in Tierra del Fuego at breakfast the next morning.

On day two, the most taciturn and earnest of the guides, Jim, agreed to teach me a bit about casting after breakfast. As one who has flunked golf and tennis and who, despite raising three sons, still throws like a girl, I was relieved that my fishing companions were too occupied with organizing their gear for the day to take notice of my initial flailing efforts. Standing there on the gravel bank, I remembered the father in Norman Maclean's *A River Runs through It* saying, "It is an art that is performed on a four-count rhythm between ten and two o'clock." I play the piano, and I can tell time. Maybe I wouldn't be a complete stooge at this after all. Nothing I had read prepared me for the sensual and seductive grace of line loading, looping, and landing so quietly on a clear stream. I emerged from this first lesson not caring if I caught fish. No wonder asking "How many?" is a secondary question for the fly fisher.

Anne, who had brought along her portable fly-tying equipment, agreed to fish with me that first day. Fortuitously, Mike, our guide, is a kindergarten teacher in the off-season. Rigged out in my lumpy borrowed neoprene chest waders with shoulder straps rolled around my waist, I looked like an overgrown toddler with a loaded diaper. My heavy wading boots felt like something Neil Armstrong would have worn on the moon, but without his advantage of weightlessness. I was certain that I would need Mike's Mister Rogers patience. I was also confident that Anne, a university teacher with strong opinions on education, would be able to provoke a rise in our boat even if the wily trout eschewed her carefully tied and "matched" golden stone flies in the river. The day would not be dull.

Anne fished quite independently from the front of the boat, and I took the swivel seat strapped onto the back. My feet didn't reach the boat floor, so Mike made me wear a life jacket, which was wise since at midday, when he bumped our boat into a rocky shoal, I slid right off my perch into the cold but fortunately shallow water. The promised rhythm, elegance, and grace would not be mine that day. Mike, probably forewarned that there were lawyers in our group, was wildly apologetic and solicitous. He had a Band-Aid on my bloody finger almost before I saw the scrape. The sun was high, and my wet clothes really didn't feel half bad, but I accepted his offer of a spare cotton windbreaker while my sopping shirt dried quickly in the clear mountain air.

Less than an hour later, I unintentionally evened the score with Mike by hooking him in the cheek with my golden stone fly imitator. He is bearded, so I never knew if I had scarred him for life. Anne expertly extracted the hook, and Mike acted as if this was part of his job description. Still, my eagerness to cast from the boat, especially in the wind that had risen, was greatly diminished.

Mike pulled up on a weedy island bank and placed me at a safe distance from all living things to practice casting upstream and slowly stripping in my line. I regained a little confidence and surprised myself by actually catching two small brown trout. Later in the afternoon, when we again anchored near a promising creek (pronounced "crick" in Montana), I was content to sit on the bank and watch the serious artistry of Alan, the most intense member of the party, as he waded in to work the riffles and fishy pools. When I accused him of being Brad Pitt's stuntman in *A River Runs through It,* he modestly replied, "Yeah, I put ice cubes in his glass for him."

Dinner was more convivial this second night. We all had stories from the day to tell, and frankly, having tried to fish, I was a little more interested in their endless tales of fishing in New Zealand with elkhair caddis and humpies. We were developing the sort of "friends of the road" camaraderie that comes with a few days of no showers and no mirrors. The four men that I didn't know before—Walt, Alan, Ramsay, and George— were no longer just generic fishing gear guys with their noses buried in Jon Krakauer best-sellers. I learned their wives' names, a little about their grown children, and a lot about their diverse business experiences, which ran the gamut from flowers, mushrooms, sunscreens, and grocery store chains to magazine distribution, real estate, and wool production.

The third morning on the river, I pronounced it too cold to fish. Not surprisingly, my opinion carried no weight. We had sixty miles of river to cover, and unscheduled dawdling would mean we'd be overtaken by fishing parties a day behind us. In the cold, gray mist, I sat defiantly in the prow of our boat, bundled into most of the clothes I'd brought. My husband, John, my fishing companion for the morning, reiterated that I didn't have to do anything on this trip I didn't want to, so I crammed my hat low on my forehead and attempted the new *New Yorker* cryptogram puzzle that I conveniently kept stuffed in one of my fishing vest pockets. A half mile downstream, the sun broke through, and I felt uncomfortably like a spoiled Cleopatra being borne with great braking effort slowly down a swift-flowing Nile. I asked for a Madame X nymph and rejoined the fishing party.

Brian was so expert in maneuvering our boat that I actually felt my placement of flies was improving. In retrospect, I am certain that he anticipated my miscasting and positioned the boat so that my line floated close to the cliff wall or near the weedy bank. I caught no fish that morning, but the boat guide's praise of my improving skills was so fulsome that I could hardly wait to get back on the river after our picnic lunch. My fishing companions changed twice daily. My new friends, the four men, were unfailingly courteous. Since none of them felt obliged to lecture me on the etiquette of this sport, I rewarded their good manners by earnestly ensnarling their lines and spoiling their fishiest opportunities with my novice flogging. Jim, the always gentlemanly friend who had invited us all on the trip, said midweek, "Well, I knew the men would be clamoring to fish with you, Prudence." Sure. I was being handed off like the Queen of Spades in a game of Old Maid. I was frankly relieved when one of them lost his cool and yelled, "For God's sake, Prudence, stop that sidearm casting if you're going to sit up front."

I fished like a woman possessed that afternoon. I cast by the sheer wall, now by the bank, into the eddy, just behind that rock, back to the sandstone cliff, then into the riffle. It began to rain and the temperature dropped. The wind came up. Still I fished. I tied a dozen wind knots in my line. My arm got so tired that I had to stand up in the boat and get my whole body into the act to cast any distance. Despite my persistent efforts, I was always stunned when a fish took my fly. So accustomed to hooking weeds, the boat rope, the guide, or a rock, I instinctively apologized the instant I felt resistance on my line. The guide pronounced my two fish "nice browns." I never heard of anyone catching a naughty brown or an ugly rainbow.

The rain and sheer exhaustion finally forced us to take shelter in our camp. I was shocked to realize that it was nearly eight o'clock. I had fished nonstop for more than eight hours. My husband, who had been fishing with Jim, showed up an hour later. Clearly, not only the novice had become obsessed. John was too wet, cold, and tired to leave the tent for the stuffed-mushroom appetizers and the enormous plate of chicken parmigiana that our exhausted guides cooked up for our dinner. The rest of us ate with chattering teeth. The wind whipped our dining room tarpaulin about and threatened to collapse the oars that staked the cooking-area tarp.

I was up before anyone else the next morning. While I washed my face in the cold, clear river, a stately flock of Canadian geese paddling by in the clear dawn light gave me a brief eyes-right acknowledgment, but no honking.

This fly-fishing trip was so much more than catching and releasing fish. After a breakfast of blueberry pancakes around a fire, we hiked a steep rise to a breathtaking yellow meadow, then down to Tenderfoot Creek, which provided the best day of wade fishing for most of the party. The hiking uphill and straight down was fairly arduous, and I was rather proud of myself for making it. I hope no one has a picture of me being carried piggyback the last five yards by one of the young guides. I could have made it. I just didn't want to ruin my new hiking boots in the marshy approach to the creek. Tenderfoot proved too swift for my short legs to cross, so I spent much of the day watching the others disappear around bends in the clear stream. Anne, who is taller, managed the current quite well with a nifty and remarkably sturdy walking stick that she magically retrieved and quickly assembled from a pocket in her fishing vest. Fly fishers have endlessly surprising resources tucked away in their many pockets.

I fished the remaining days with little success by a fisherman's standards, but with great success by my own. I almost hooked a small, disoriented bat who dive-bombed our boat early one afternoon. I drank water from Indian Springs and tried to capture on a treble clef I drew in my notebook the melodic triad warbling and staccato of the meadowlark. I discovered that baby wipes are almost as good as a shower and won the Sacagawea look-alike contest by wadding my dirty hair into dog-ears midweek. Before Montana, I had never quite believed in the constellation Orion the Hunter. I could spot his belt, but the rest required more imagination than I could muster. Standing outside our tent at night in the last boat camp, I could swear that I saw Orion's head, arms, legs, perhaps his shoelaces.

"I'll bet your sons will be so happy that you learned to fly-fish on this trip," one of the guides said as we floated toward the takeout point at the end of the week.

"Maybe . . ."

A week after returning to Dallas, I mailed a photo of me with my Smith River fishing buddies to one of my sons in New York, whose fishing hat I had borrowed. "This is a terrible picture you sent me," he said later on the phone.

"What's wrong with it?" I asked.

"Everything. My mother is having more fun than I am."

Montana P.S.

◆

In subsequent years I have "fished" the Bitterroot, the Smith, the Boulder, a spring creek or two, and the Yellowstone. Anyone who has fished with me understands the quotation marks. Author Norman Maclean's father would avert his Presbyterian eyes out of embarrassment for any trout caught by me. And yet, like my husband, John, I am drawn each September to these western waters.

These annual five or six days among Ponderosa pines, glacier-cut cliffs, and clear blue-green fast-flowing streams in the summer or early fall are foretastes of glory divine. Once while I was catching my breath on a hike, a handsome young couple and their equally handsome golden retriever acknowledged my presence on a big flat rock, then hiked down toward the water. Not a hundred yards from me, they tossed a stick in the water for the dog, then tossed off all their clothes and dived into the chilly stream after him. After much playful splashing, they climbed out on the sunny bank and shook themselves like their retriever, creating halos as the afternoon

sun caught the flying droplets. Any lingering moisture evaporated in their spontaneous and totally unself-conscious Edenic
embrace. They pulled on their jeans, waved at me, and disappeared around the next bend. No wonder that part of Montana is called Paradise Valley.

Strangers become friends on these trips. Keeping your distance is hard when you share common affections not only
for fly-fishing, but for the beautiful places trout have always
chosen to live. And so it was with this trip to the Blackfoot,
only more so.

John and I arrived in Missoula on Monday, September 10,
2001. On the way to Northfork Crossing Lodge, our driver
pointed out a trail taken by Meriwether Lewis and his party en
route to the Blackfoot. In *Undaunted Courage,* Stephen Ambrose,
whose home is nearby, records this part of Lewis's separate
expedition through one of the most beautiful valleys in Montana as "happily uneventful." Howard, the driver, allowed us a
stop in Ovando (population: 40), which has a general store, a
post office, a bed-and-breakfast, a two-room schoolhouse. and,
of course, a fly-fishing shop. The shop is guarded by a languor-
ous basset hound named Otis, who expects a certain amount
of tummy scratching from all visitors. He was clearly irked at
the time we spent dithering over licenses and flies.

I always pore over the literature describing these trips, looking for two items that will entertain me should fishing fail.
First I look for evidence of a piano in the lodge and then the
possibility of bedside reading lamps. I confess the words "luxurious tents" made me wary. In the case of Northfork Crossing, the phrase was no oxymoron. I would have earned high-
est honors in scouting if camping out had been like this. Wood
floors, a pair of rough-hewn single beds so cozy and comfortable I couldn't call them bunks, a matching table with a small
mirror, bottled water replenished daily, an electric heater that

I could flip on before sliding out of bed each morning and—YES!!!!—a reading lamp clamped at just the right angle on the bed. Additional tenting above the tent ensured that rain would never reach us, and a pair of director's chairs on the small front porch provided perfect perches for cleaning line or just taking in the beauty of the distant mountains and the reedy stocked pond where fat trout dimpled to whet fishermen's appetites for the day's more challenging wild rivers and spring creeks. Need I mention the luxurious private (one for each tent) bathrooms not ten yards away, replete with flushing toilets, showers, hair dryers, and plenty of hot water? And finally, a pleasant stroll away in the lovely lodge the tables were set, and a real chef in the kitchen was conjuring up gourmet feasts for each evening as well as groaning boards of blueberry pancakes, pecan scones, and egg casseroles for breakfast. I could live without the piano.

Back home in Dallas, we greet the first cold snap, which rarely comes before the end of October, as "a Montana morning." To experience the real thing, that absolutely pure intake of sweet-smelling air, on September 11, with the anticipation of fishing the big river that runs through it made us downright giddy as we headed to the lodge for coffee.

As I filled my mug, however, the euphoria evaporated. The earlier risers, guests and guides, were already packed into the basement office of the lodge, their attention glued to the small TV. Here on Rocky Mountain Time, in this clear air where the morning mist had just lifted from the glistening water, we were so out of sync with the East Coast. What we were seeing for the first time on television—the first plane, then the second—had happened at least an hour earlier. It was hard to conceive of so much suffering occurring while I was breathing in the fresh beauty of the morning. Together we watched the hideous crumpling of the towers and the huge eruption of black smoke that billowed like lava through all of lower Manhattan. I bolted from the basement room, nauseated by the sudden realization that my oldest son works only blocks from the World Trade Center and often had business in the towers themselves. I hardly acknowledged the third plane hitting the Pentagon and the subsequent downing of the plane in Pennsylvania. I had to find my boy.

Cell phones generally don't work in rural Montana. That's why you go there. The two lines in the lodge could not begin to accommodate our need to reach our families and friends. I'm not sure how we queued up. Whit, our leader, had a young family in Washington, D.C. Another member of our party lived in Manhattan. The chef had worked there. Almost everyone had old school friends or business associates working in or near the towers. Miraculously, Jack answered the phone at his office. He had seen it all from his tenth-floor window. Initially seeing papers flying from windows, he'd thought it was a ticker tape parade. "Then I saw a shoe, Mom. That's when I looked up and saw the smoke coming out the top and the sudden fireball of the second hit," he told me. By the time I reached him, he already knew that bridges, subways, and tunnels were closed, and he wasn't sure how he'd get back to his apartment in Hoboken. He had to let others in his office use the phone before I could tell him how to reach me in Montana when he had a bed for the night. I later realized I had given my other sons in Dallas and Houston the outfitter's number in Helena instead of the number of the lodge. Their attempts to return my calls reached an answering machine.

Watching repeats of the horror on television in the basement only increased our frustrating sense of powerlessness, so we reluctantly geared up for what should have been one of the great days of our lives. The guides were ready to go, lunches were packed, and boats were waiting. I was a good sport all morning, hoping that attending to "God's four count rhythm" while floating the Blackfoot could somehow put things right again, or at least distract me for a few hours. I caught one small trout on a Royal Wulff. I think he felt sorry for me. By noon it had warmed up, however, and my waders were hot, and fishing, even here in Paradise, seemed akin to fiddling while Rome burned. Untying wind knots could no longer distract me. I really didn't know that my son was safe. Debris was surely falling from the wreckage, and perhaps even his building was weakened by the tremors from the collapse of buildings so close. I put away my rod and cried quietly behind my polarized glasses until the takeout point. I wanted to go home.

Much has been written about where we find comfort at times like this. Retrieving the messages on my home phone, I was struck by the number of dear friends who remembered that I had a son near those towers. One from Maryland said, "If your son Jack is part of this, I will ride a bicycle if necessary to meet you in New York." The messages were consoling. I didn't erase them.

Comfort also came from strangers. A cascade of infectious female laughter erupted from the kitchen, and one of the helpers explained that Renee, a former owner of the lodge, had stopped by to help peel potatoes. With her came three stray dogs from the local SPCA, for which she is always seeking adoptions. Dogs, especially multicolored mutts of indistinguishable breed, are so obviously in need of love and affection that one's own human anxieties are momentarily obscured by the flurry of tail wagging and oafish romping. Renee's easy laugh and her oblivious canine entourage momentarily diverted us from the somber scene emanating from the basement television.

None of the books I'd brought on this trip gave much solace. (No Gideon Bibles in the luxury tents!) My husband had brought Walter Kirn's satirical novel on airline travel, *Up in the Air.* The minor indignities of our airport lives suddenly seemed minor indeed. Waiting in line for the phone again and again, I perused the award-winning photographic essay by Laura Wilson, *Hutterites of Montana,* lying on the lodge table. What had seemed yesterday to be a record of a weird Montana sect more isolated than the Amish or the Mennonites today had seductive appeal. The persistence of Wilson, who spent fourteen years patiently gaining the trust of these gentle people who shun worldly vanity, especially the vanity of a photograph, was inspiring. Looking at page after page of their serene faces had a calming effect as the latest life-shattering news filtered in from our beloved technology. These rural Hutterite lives attuned to a simple rhythm of hard work and prayerful gratitude so lovingly documented made the syncopated staccato patterns of hurried urban lives lived in vertical towers seem very distant.

The next morning, needing a break from the telephone that couldn't seem to locate my son, I hiked a couple of miles up the road behind our campsite. Bright purple thistle and the surrounding blue mountains relieved the bleakness of the dry early-fall landscape. A bird or two, never an airplane, and the rhythmic crunch of my hiking boots on gravel broke the almost reverential silence. The soothing cadences of the King James Psalms, memorized during a Bible Belt childhood, welled up: "I will lift up mine eyes unto the hills. From whence cometh my help? . . . He will not suffer thy foot to be moved; . . . The sun shall not smite thee by day, nor the moon by night. . . . The Lord shall preserve thy going out and thy coming in from this time forth, and even for evermore." The psalmist who longed to be led by "still waters," of course, could not have been a trout fisherman.

The fourteen or so of us gathered for dinner that night

were glad that Peg said that immutable Episcopal grace that always seems to cover the proper territory: "Bless, O Lord, this food to our use, and us to thy loving and faithful service, and make us mindful of the needs of others. Amen." Some things hadn't changed. Good fishermen exchanged their stories of effectual flies, great stretches of water, beautiful cutthroats, and fat browns. I think most were a little relieved, however, that the next day would be devoted to touring conservation projects that benefit anglers, farmers, ranchers, fish, and the waters they all share. If we couldn't give blood, a communal endeavor seemed in order on September 12.

My call from Jack finally came through. His building had been evacuated around 3 P.M. the day of the tragedy. With wet paper towels on their faces, he and his coworkers had hiked north to a Twenty-second Street pier, where they found a Coast Guard boat willing to ferry them to New Jersey. He was physically okay. The exhaustion in his voice, however, made me reluctant to press for any more detail.

Assured of the safety of immediate friends and family, but still strangely separated from the suffering of the country, we sang a verse of "America, the Beautiful" outside after dinner. There is certain solace for city dwellers in a Montana Milky Way and a fully articulated Orion the Hunter.

Fishing the remaining two days of the trip was fraught with ambivalence. With my husband and patient guide Dan, I clambered over barbed-wire fences in my lumpy waders, sidestepped cow patties, trekked through forests noticing flora and butterflies I'd never seen before, forded pristine waters, stalked, caught, and, of course, released a wily cutthroat. I longed to be home, and then again, I didn't. My son was safe, but I was certain that someone I knew probably wasn't. Concerns about airline travel collided with the absurd idea that we felt so safe right here in the wild. Like the trout, some part of us wanted to remain here, feeding comfortably on the "edge of the swirls."

But, "eventually," as the Maclean who knew the Blackfoot more intimately than we ever will, wrote, "all things merge into one." We bade our fishing buddies farewell with fierce hugs and surrendered our cuticle nippers to security at the Missoula airport. When we landed in Salt Lake City on our return to Dallas, my little red cell phone, dormant for almost a week, sprang to life. All of the urgent messages logged on September 11 from my children spewed forth in frantic succession:

"Mom, Dad, it's 8:17 here. Two planes have crashed into the World Trade Center. I've tried to call Jack. Call me if you've reached him."

"Mom, Dad . . . pick up your phone. Things are out of control. I can't find Jack."

"Mom, Dad, where the hell are you? I've called the number you left. It's an answering machine. I still don't know about Jack."

"Mom, Dad, I've talked to Jack. He's okay, but still in his building. Please call when you get this message."

We are haunted relentlessly now by the events of September 11, but in some ways grateful that the news came to us in a place that buffered despair. It is hard to feel that things in this world are utterly changed when "a river still runs through it over rocks from the basement of time."

A Disclaimer
for My Daughter-in-Law
(If I Ever Have One)

◆

Nothing brings a mother of sons more feelings of things left undone than the thought of handing one of them off to another woman. Perhaps if I'd done my job better, I'd already have a daughter-in-law in my life. Do the wet towels mildewing on the floor of their apartments drive you away? Or is it the empty toilet tissue roll with no spare in sight? The toothpaste-encrusted bathroom sink? The little piles of used Kleenex, gum wrappers, Post-it notes, and pocket change that accumulate on every flat surface? It drives me nuts, too.

Give them a second look. They're out of diapers, bathe, and brush their teeth regularly. They do their own laundry. Two of the three can fold clothes better than I can. One can iron. (I'm sworn to secrecy.) Yes, I know, one just pulls what he needs from the clean pile in the corner. All of them can cook breakfast, steam broccoli, boil pasta, and grill a hamburger. The one who irons also does excellent yard work. I have never packed a suitcase for any of them.

Such résumé details, however, only suggest a certain self-sufficiency, a hope that they will not be a burden to those around them. The larger question is whether my influence in this all-male household was sufficient to instill respect for and understanding of women. They respect *me*, but that wasn't the assignment. I worry that I have given them a very skewed, minimalist idea of what women are like and what they expect.

I am by temperament and upbringing a low-maintenance woman. Writing at home doesn't require a lot of clothes. I have never felt the need to hide extravagant retail purchases in my closet or the trunk of the car, as I know some women do. I have no gift closet in which to store items to give as spontaneous gifts for friends. I never believed one size fit all. I have no collectibles other than a handful of books signed by authors whom I greatly admire.

If the fashion magazine articles that I read in doctors' waiting rooms are any indication, I've done an exceedingly poor job of preparing my sons for the expensive beauty regimens that seem to be standard for women today. With a son in tow, I once sat at a counter at Henri Bendel's in New York letting a makeup artist transform me. My son thought it was hilarious. "This is so weird. My mother never does this," he kept saying a bit apologetically to passersby. As the cosmetics salesperson totaled up the products my transformation required, my customary indulgence of eight good haircuts a year and drugstore lipsticks seemed by comparison like a Lenten discipline. That a woman might also require regular and costly hair coloring, eyelash dyeing, waxing, collagen injections, massages, nail applications, pedicures, liposuction, and spa visits . . . well, don't hit my boys with this all at once.

I've never cared about jewelry the way many women do. Since my husband was still in law school when we married, we agreed on no debts for an engagement ring. I happily wore a simple gold band. Twenty years later, when he wanted to buy me a diamond ring for our anniversary, I surprised him, however, by rejecting the first stones offered as "too small." Well, this is Texas.

The roses purchased at a roadside stand for two dollars a dozen by my tired lawyer husband driving home from a deposition in Tyler, Texas, always made my heart sing, especially when he splurged and bought ten dollars' worth. He is even lower maintenance than I am. We've never carried a balance on a credit card, and since we first married, our joint incomes have always been deposited to a single checking account. Awareness of what we can and cannot afford has been, for us, an effortless calculation.

My most extravagant indulgence is the 1931 Steinway piano that I purchased with book earnings in 1981. I do not think there are any women in my sons' lives who would long for and happily receive new piano bushings for their fiftieth birthdays.

Low-maintenance moms fit comfortably into male households, where shopping is neither a recreational outing nor a bonding experience. The only regular shopping that such mothers do is to replace items that have been lost, broken, torn, or eaten. Boys require only two pairs of shoes. Beyond having the prescribed suitably distressed jeans, they never worry much about what is in their closets. Guys rarely give each other gifts. Once zits are banished, their grooming requires about four items. Their idea of decorating their rooms in their teenage years is a beer can collection pyramid and a *Sports Illustrated* swimsuit calendar. Spend twenty-five years in this environment and your God-given female ability to sweat the small stuff is greatly impaired.

I realize, of course, that I am not the measure of all things female. For many years, however, I had to be the interpreter. Girls intruded in their lives long before they were ready to take much notice. One early phone conversation went something like this:

"William? Do you like Sarah?"

"Nope, who is this?"

"Do you like Alice?"

"Nope."

Getting nowhere, the young lady changed her tactics. "William, I'm going to name five girls. If you like any of them, just say 'yes.'"

My boy was totally baffled by this conversation, but I recognized the ploy. One simple scrap of a "yes" from the uninterested male could fuel the romantic speculations of all five preteen girls attending the slumber party. I tried to translate complicated female behavior for my sons, but in a house where talk about *feelings* once veered off into a discussion of dental *fillings,* I made little headway.

They were frequently puzzled by girls' questions. They still relegate certain female queries to the category "Up or Down," an allusion to a time in the fifth grade when a girl asked my eldest son if he liked her hair up in a ponytail or down. He was struck dumb by the question. Was he supposed to have an opinion on that? I occasionally forget where I live and ask similar questions of my menfolk about a new lipstick color. They respond, "I don't know, Mom. Up or down, I guess." They have promised to tell me, when I'm in my dotage, if I'm going around looking like a clown, with too much cheek color, but I'm not sure I can trust them.

A father of three girls once asked me, "How did you find time to write books? All of my wife's energies were devoted to engineering the girls' social lives."

In high school boys would have no social lives if the girls' mothers didn't do this elaborate planning and engineering. Would the boys miss it? Probably not. This arranged social world is fraught with complexities and underlying agendas that boys don't understand. Most boys don't think about or even mention an invitation until it's almost too late to rent a tux or order flowers. I once saw them work up the courage to ask a girl to a required social engagement by making a game of the asking. Five guy friends made up lists of "off the wall" words and bet money that nobody could use all five words in the conversation with the girl. Surrounded by witnesses, the victim received his list ("panties, goalpost, bicycle, throat, carburetor") the moment the girl answered the phone. The sting of rejection could at least be mitigated by winning the pool of money.

If they did get dates, they worried that sending flowers might send messages they didn't intend. "Do these flowers we're supposed to send before the homecoming dance represent a lot of commitment?" This sounds like the cover of a women's magazine, but I thought a moment and advised, "Well, I think sending roses is bit more romantic than sending cut flowers in the school colors." "I think I'll get her the school colors," he said with some relief. "Do you think they'll wilt by Tuesday?" Was this the day he planned to break up with her? Was I an accomplice?

Sometimes my advice is apparently off the mark. "Is the first week of December too late to break up with a girl?" a son once asked. "I mean, is it going to look like I just didn't want to give her a present?" I responded confidently, "Look, girls want you to be honest. Regardless of the time of year, they would surely find it humiliating to be with someone who was just pretending because of some perceived obligation." Later, I compared notes with female friends on this and was shocked by their swift reproach. "Absolutely not! He can't break up in December. What is he thinking? She's already bought her clothes for the parties. I remember a guy tried to break up with me before the holidays. I told him that he could just do all of this in January, but he was damn sure not copping out now. We got through New Year's Eve. I didn't miss a single party, and he dumped me in January." Maybe I need more estrogen.

Living in a house with no other females has occasionally been isolating and frustrating, but I have to admit I was well suited for it. I grew up with a brother, and as the mother of sons, I was allowed to continue my lifelong membership in the "No Girls Allowed Club." The benefit of this membership is the understanding of the male psyche it brings. The downside is that one grows accustomed to the laconic speech, the no-frills simplicity, the guileless honesty, the slapstick vulgar comedy of boys and begins to view her own gender with disloyal objectivity. My friends who only have sons tell me I am not alone in this accommodation. Thrust into an all-female environment, such as the Dallas Women's Club or a breast cancer fund-raiser, mothers of sons can often be found hiding in the rest room. Suddenly encountering the higher-pitched shriek of several hundred Texas women in a hotel atrium sends us straight to the stalls to rearrange our antennae. The frequency signals in this crowd are initially unfamiliar. We emerge from consummate girly affairs, a wedding shower or an exquisite tea party, wondering if we've completely lost our feminine credentials.

As comfortable as the No Girls Allowed Club is, for civility's sake I cannot in good faith abet my sons' natural inclination to flee from the "constraining qualities of grace" that women impose. And yet, mothers of sons are often enablers. We rent the tux and purchase the date's flowers for them, and after reviewing a basic list of manners that we have encouraged, but not always enforced at home, we shove them out the door.

A young female friend looked on one afternoon as I neatly

wrapped a gift that one teenage son would later give to his girlfriend. She remarked, "I never knew that mothers of boys did the wrapping."

"The wrapping? Who do you think selected the gift?" I said, wondering if I should invite her in some Christmas morning to see the caliber of gift swaddling that my sons offer. By overruling my teenage son's impulse to give his best girl a Blockbuster gift certificate, I like to think I am teaching him something about what might please a woman. Perhaps I have only taught him that gift selection is beyond him. That was not my intention.

In a household of males, the teaching cannot be subtle. Take something as basic as "Women would like to be remembered on their birthdays." It doesn't take long in a houseful of males to know that you have to post the date on the refrigerator early. Once they all could read and write, I instructed my husband to back off. No more purchasing the card for them and extracting the signatures. (They always signed their last names, as if the card might be used in court.)

That first year of my "Let's see how thoughtful they are on their own" experiment was a disaster. As my birthday approached, each time the older two left the house, I bade them farewell by saying, "I know you're really going to buy your mother's birthday present, but you can pretend that you're going to play video games if you want to." The eldest, in a moment of real martyrdom, promised he would accompany me to church, since my birthday fell on Sunday. The day arrived, and he, of course, woke up late and mumbled that he would come in his own car. He was a no-show.

Returning from church, I fixed Sunday lunch and waded into the pile of laundry that invariably accumulates on weekends. Any boy who passed me in the hall heard me remark that my car needed washing and I would consider that a lovely birthday gift. The son who skipped church was nervy enough to ask for help in using my computer. He probably didn't even hear my teeth grinding as I sat beside him. At five o'clock I baked myself a birthday cake, which they happily consumed. Later that evening, I exploded on all of them, including hapless William, who had just returned from a weekend Scout campout.

I told them that I didn't want to be misunderstood, so I would not be speaking to them subtly or metaphorically. I would not infer or imply. "I AM HURT!" I told them that I felt totally unappreciated and rather lousy as a parent who had brought up such thoughtless males. (Note how quickly I began to assume responsibility for their failure.) My wrath seemed to take them entirely by surprise. I saw that fuzzy look come into their eyes that says, "What is she talking about? What is it with women? What does she want?"

They averted their eyes, so I grabbed their chins the way I once did when they were errant toddlers with three-second attention spans. "What do I want? I'll tell you what I want and you'd better listen up because this is what all women want. I want to be surprised, not by a lavish gift, but by evidence that someone observed and loved me enough to know what would lighten my load and brighten my day. My car is filthy, for starters. Your insistence on taking over the Sunday laundry chore would delight me, even if you didn't sort the clothes. Somebody could make me a cake. A cake mix is fine. You can all read and set the oven at 350 degrees. The two of you who went to church with me heard me exclaim over the John Rutter 'Requiem' on the way home. I think I even wondered aloud if it might be available on compact disk IN THE CLASSICAL SECTION OF THE MUSIC STORE. Your mother writes. She never tires of nice paper and interesting pens. I didn't even mind the year that you collectively decided that I wanted a Whitman

Sampler box of candy, except that you ate the best pieces and left the lid off the box on a low table so that Rosie devoured the rest and threw up all night in the living room."

The blindsided youngest ran to his room and returned with an offering of his much prized "fake snot." The middle child kicked at the carpet and said, "Sorry I blew it, Mom." Still in the throes of adolescent rebellion, the hardheaded eldest, who has been with me longest and consequently retains the greatest capacity to wound, provided the capper for the day. Returning to his homework on my computer, he said over his shoulder, "You can draw some money out of my savings account tomorrow and get yourself something nice." I retired to the front porch, howled at the full moon and had a good cry.

In subsequent years, all they seemed to retain from this scorched-earth display was the Whitman Sampler idea. I must have been too effusive the year it was bestowed, giving them the idea that they had this gift-giving stuff knocked. Apparently, this is the way the male brains in my house work: If she liked the gift last year, she'll like it again next year. At least they remembered to put the chocolates out of the dog's reach. Their Christmas gifts to me became similarly predictable. Although I can't remember expressing any affection for the artist, I inexplicably received Norman Rockwell wall calendars. One year they waited too late to get the Norman Rockwell and had to settle for Native Americans. Mothers of sons eventually slip into thinking such behavior is somehow endearing. I know their wives will not.

Tears, of course, are the teaching tool of last resort. My sons are confused, frightened, and repelled by them. I hope I used them sparingly enough to retain their effectiveness. All of my boys learned to recognize what they called "the cry point" and cautioned each other to back off before the dam broke. I acknowledge that I contributed to the confusion, however. Once, many years ago, after I had retired to the bathroom to repair my tearstained face, a consequence of some infuriating thoughtlessness on their part, one of my three knocked on the door to make amends. In his small hand was a little tin box with a messaged taped to the top. He had intended to write, "It's for you, Mom," but in his first-grade dyslexic scrawl it came out more poetically, "*Tis* for you, Mom." Inside was his treasured Eisenhower silver dollar. To his utter bewilderment, his gift brought more tears.

The tears of other women in their lives have probably been more instructive than mine. One son confessed that during an emotional farewell after a summer romance, he felt so bad about his inability to cry with her that he licked his fingers when she wasn't looking and made streaks on his cheeks.

If they found Gift Giving 101 and tears so baffling, I despaired of their ever understanding that women would also like a little romance. They, of course, thought that my advice was absurdly dated. John and I offered counsel from an era when men had to take risks and do the pursuing, when nice girls not only *didn't,* they didn't even call.

I still think it's instructive to tell my sons our corny courtship story: John was dating my beautiful blond roommate, who broke his heart by saying one evening, "You should go out with Prudence. You're too smart for me." We met six months later at a wedding. He was the groomsman who took me down the aisle of the church where we married three years later. Noting that I had come to the wedding unescorted, he seated me and whispered, "If you'd like a ride to the reception, I can take you." We danced the night away at the reception, and after too much champagne, he lectured me on the rise of the right wing in American politics. The next day he drove to Mexico with an old friend, to whom he confided that he had met the girl he intended to marry.

My groom, who still calls me "Great Beauty," employed a lot of imagination in that 1960s courtship. Once I found a cryptic note in my college dorm mailbox: "Contact a man named Jace in the basement of the University Co-op. He will instruct you further." The man named Jace, a student clerk at the campus bookstore, handed me a matchbook with some rhyming lines scribbled in the cover, something about "the source of wisdom holds your next clue." After some puzzling, I remembered a statue of Athena in the backyard of my sorority house. Propped in her hands was a small portable radio with another message attached, something about "Bring this with you. The play's the thing wherein we'll catch the conscience of the king . . . James, that is. The next clue was biblical, but the "James" also had a 007 meaning, since James Bond movies were all the rage. I was not romantic or sentimental enough to have saved all of the clever clues, but I remember that the game all ended with his waiting for me in Eastwood Park beside his faded blue VW bug with a picnic. "A loaf of bread, a jug of wine, and thou?" No, we weren't that corny.

My sons maintain that this is all fabrication. They think that I won their father as a consolation prize in a poker game with Elizabeth, lovely blond roommate who became their godmother. Despite daily evidence to the contrary, they refuse to believe that the man who embarrasses them by standing in the front yard watering the dogwoods with his boxer shorts hanging beneath his Bermuda shorts can ever have been the perpetrator of such romantic devotion.

These young men are no longer under my roof. If I wince at occasional jerky boy behavior that remains, I also glory in their sporadic grown-up thoughtfulness. They have always been funny and spontaneously affectionate. The Whitman Samplers no longer appear on my birthday. Even the bookstore gift certificates, which are always welcome in my house, have been replaced by a genuine effort to locate a book I've been longing for or, better yet, one they found provocative and worthy of discussion. They know the power of flowers to cheer and disarm a woman; they even know *not* to send the standard FTD bouquet. Aside from the hilarious practical jokes they inflict on her, they are attentive to their surviving grandmother, Jane. They learned to listen patiently to their grandfather's genuinely funny tales (funny the first time, at least) of life and love as he knew it in the twenties. After what seems like decades of forced thank-you notes, I am certain that they know that life requires gratitude. They can offer it now with wit and grace. If this has been long in coming, I beg forgiveness. Remember how outnumbered I was in this good ol' boy locker room.

None of my boys has found a wife yet. At the weddings of my friends' children, I sometimes fantasize about what it will be like to be the mother of the groom. Yes, I know the groom's mother wears beige and keeps her mouth shut. I used to worry about which of the remaining two sons I would choose to take me down the aisle until another mother of three boys solved it for me by making a regal entrance on the arms of two sons. In my fantasy, once seated, I float somewhere on the organ prelude above the candles and the flowers, near the vaulted cathedral ceiling until the groom marches in with his best man. His smile brings me back to earth. Oh, the times we have seen together! Now framed in a grown-up face, this is the smile I saw when his first tooth came out, the smile of the successful goalie on the soccer field, the dazzling smile when the braces came off, the thumbs-up smile he flashed when he finally got his driver's license, the unself-conscious pick-me-up-and-swing-me-around smile at the airport gate on holiday returns from college. I wink and acknowledge his smile. But, wait—his smile is beaming just over my left shoulder, beyond me up the aisle, expectantly, adoringly, as it should be. For her.